THE
PERPETUAL
MOTION
MACHINE

T0165780

THE PERPETUAL MOTION MACHINE

A MEMOIR

Brittany Ackerman

Red Hen Press | *Pasadena, CA*

Book layout by Mark E. Cull

ISBN: 978-1-59709-691-1

Library of Congress Control Number: 2018032432

The National Endowment for the Arts, the Los Angeles County Arts Commission, the Dwight Stuart Youth Fund, the Max Factor Family Foundation, the Pasadena Tournament of Roses Foundation, the Pasadena Arts & Culture Commission and the City of Pasadena Cultural Affairs Division, the City of Los Angeles Department of Cultural Affairs, the Audrey & Sydney Irmas Charitable Foundation, the Ahmanson Foundation, the Meta & George Rosenberg Foundation, the Kinder Morgan Foundation, the Allergan Foundation, the Riordan Foundation, and the Amazon Literary Partnership partially support Red Hen Press.

First Edition
Published by Red Hen Press
www.redhen.org

Acknowledgments

The story, "Space Mountain," first appeared in *No Tokens* Issue No. 7 in 2018.

To my mother, for always being there and helping us through.

Contents

THE
PERPETUAL
MOTION
MACHINE

Fire Drill

My mat is in the middle of the room. I usually prefer an edge, a wall to run my hands and feet up and down, to make like an upside-down candlestick and pretend to drip, drip. But today I have to make a home for Snowman. Snowman is a stuffed toy with a red crown. He's from some book I've never read. I hate his crown because it's made of felt. I've tried to rip it off, but my brother says he'd look weird without it. He has yellow buttons down his middle, but his hands and feet are my favorite. They are large and puffy and I suck on them sometimes. I bite his flesh and small strings of fluff stick to the roof of my mouth. He's not here with me on my mat. We are only allowed one toy at rest time. I've chosen a set of silk paintings I made in St. Martin. I have four, and I can fashion a makeshift house with three walls and a roof. I set up the foundation as I've done many times before.

Snowman is in my backpack, and if I pretend to go to the bathroom, I can sneak there and get him, bring him back to my mat, rescue him from the nothingness of the inside of my school bag. I never rest at rest time and I don't understand the kids who do. My best friend, Gillian Price, has been moved away from me for talking too much or else she'd put her Ellie the Elephant inside my house. I don't like it when she does that because Snowman needs his own place, a space to keep him warm. I can hear her on the other side of the room talking to Greer Goldbloom. I can't hear what they're saying, just girlish whispers thin as baby hairs. I focus on my house. It really is a beautiful house; the silk paintings are done in bright blues, golds, greens, and purples, my favorites.

The walls of the house keep falling down and I pick them back up. I can't get the structure right today. I think about Snowman's face, his dumb happy face in my bag. I think about my mom picking me up from school and giving me a milk box and then I feel a little sick, like I need her here. Matthew Zimpkin is asleep next to me and his sleeve is covered in snot. He is sick and maybe I've caught his sickness. I wonder if he's even still alive in his navy blue turtleneck. I hold one of the silk paintings to my face, the one with the fish in the middle that the lady at the hotel in St. Martin traced for me. All I had to do was color it in with the paint. Gold, orange, black, blue, purple. The eyes are done in purple. I remember the way the paint bled into the silk.

I drift off and dream about St. Martin. The year we went there instead of Aruba, our usual vacation spot. The heat in the middle of December, a family vacation for the winter holiday, the way Santa came down in a helicopter and gave all the kids presents. He was wearing a bathing suit. All

the kids ran toward him and his bag of toys. He was waving at us, smiling, sweating. I was sweating too, my hair
sticking to my forehead, my shorts sticking to my thighs,
and my brother was running, faster than me to receive his
gift from the fake Santa. It was so hot, and I kept thinking
about how we were Jewish and shouldn't even get presents.
And I wake up on my mat and everyone is gone. Matthew,
Gillian, Greer, my teacher. Everyone is gone and I'm on my
mat, face down and sweating in my purple sweater. My ears
hurt and my eyes water. A fire alarm is muffled but I hear
it, the way it stops and starts again. I need to leave. I have
to get outside.

I leave my mat, I leave the silk paintings, I leave my backpack with Snowman, I leave my whole life behind in that
room. I do not want to die in pre-kindergarten. I run out
the side door of the classroom that leads to the playground,
then down the big hill to where everyone is lined up ac-
cording to age and teacher. I see my group, a wave of Velcro
shoes and ankle socks. The kids look tired and confused
like me, but I'm on fire. My body is burning. I look down
the way and see the fourth graders, my brother's group. I
see a boy in denim pants, a brown turtleneck to match his
chestnut hair, clean sneakers on his feet. I see my brother
and I start to run toward him. His hands are in his pockets
and he looks out at the older kids, into the stretch of youths
beyond, down, down the massive hill. I am stopped by my
teacher, her hands gathering me into her long knit skirt,
the black curls on her head shaking, holding me back. I

am reaching for my brother. I am reaching and my teacher pulls me away. She feels my warm little body, my head in flames, she tugs at a purple sleeve to feel my clammy hands, she tells another teacher to take me away, and I am crying now, hard, and it hurts the back of my throat.

My brother turns to face up the hill and I see his eyes, brown like two chocolate chips, and I can't tell if he sees me. I am screaming, "Skyler! Sky! Sky!" at the top of my lungs and it echoes against the fire alarm. The kids will not remember. The teachers will forget it too. And maybe it didn't happen this way, any of it. Maybe I was still dreaming on my mat. But my brother remembers the day at the fire drill when his sister was left alone in her pre-K classroom and her teacher dragged her away as she screamed and cried and begged for him. He will remember it forever because it is burned in his mind. He is the brother and he must carry these things.

You Can Fly

She takes a package of Goldfish out of her purse when the ride starts. The three of us, my brother, my mom, and myself, are all packed into a fake little ship on the Peter Pan ride in Disney World. It's the same thing every time. We wait for the takeoff, we put our tiny hands out like cups, we collect the Goldfish crackers from Mom to throw at various scenes on the ride, letting them land where they fall, hoping we will come back and see them next time. This is how we create memories, something to look forward to, something to look back on.

Skyler can throw them the farthest. He gets the fish in intricate places. He knows the best spots to hide our memories. I stick to the small scenes, leaning down to plop a fish right next to the mermaids. The orange body is obvious, out in the open next to a bikini-clad mermaid sunning herself, long blond hair down her back, a starfish behind her ear.

The "You Can Fly" song plays and our ship flies along. Captain Hook captures Wendy. The Lost Boys fight to save her. Peter Pan saves the day. Captain Hook straddles a crocodile with a tick-tock in his tummy. Ripples of color represent struggle in the water. It's been this way since before I was born. His legs shake as the mouth opens and closes. Our fish are already decaying into the interior of the ride. Soon an attendant will sweep them up and curse the kids who threw them. We can only hope that one of the little snacks might get lost in the ride forever without being noticed, without any attention paid to it, slipping free between scenes and landing on the floor out of view.

When the flying ship lands, we exit the ride and Mom shoves the bag back in her purse. "We'll come back in a year and see if they're still there." Mom smiles, and even though she knows they won't be, that the ride gets cleaned and the Goldfish will be thrown away, a part of her believes they might stay, they might make it until then. When we go back and they're gone, she insists it was too dark to see, and when we replace them again, we give ourselves another year, another trip, more time to believe our own lies.

The Big Apple

Skyler loves how New York stands alone on the map. It stands out even though it's awkwardly shaped and smaller in comparison to most other states. We can see the New York skyline from our apartment in Riverdale. We live on the tenth floor of the building, high enough to see the skyscrapers far away in the city and the Hudson River close to us. We stand outside on the terrace and watch the top of the Empire State Building change its colors every few months with the seasons and the holidays. Skyler and I throw plastic army men off of our balcony and watch them parachute into the pool downstairs. I like to watch them fall, little green guys hitting a swimmer in the head, and we laugh.

One winter, our terrace becomes infested with pigeons. It gets so bad that Mom says it reminds her of Alfred Hitchcock's *The Birds*. Dad puts on oven mitts and boots to climb outside and swat them away with a broomstick. We all watch from inside. The birds must be attracted to something, finding solace on our balcony, huddling in some warmth that our terrace provides. The birds eventually leave, but their feathers remain.

In the dining room there is a window that faces the sun. Skyler places his science project of a plant growing through a maze on the windowsill. When he is at school, I hold my breath and see if it moves. I water it for him, probably too much; I want to see if it will grow, if the experiment works, if something crazy like that could really happen right before my eyes.

We take trips to Toys "R" Us on the weekends. The closest one is thirty minutes away, and on the drive there, we can't see the sign until we go under an overpass. Then, all of a sudden, it appears as if by magic and we scream. Skyler runs off by himself once we get inside. He's allowed to; he's older. Mom accompanies me to the Barbie aisle to pick out a new outfit for my doll, while Skyler goes right to the Lego section. He must have over five hundred Lego sets, but he always wants more. He loves building them on the weekends. He gets a new one on Saturday morning and finishes it by Sunday night. He stays up all night, posing each character perfectly, making sure the pieces move and glide the way they're supposed to, even spends time painting colorful and detailed accents onto the people in the set.

He has a collection of Lego people heads, one for every occasion. He has everything from an angry pirate face to a damsel in distress face. He also has a box of spare parts and random things like swords, masks, shiny coins. I steal his Lego treasure chests and collect coins to go inside them. I like to open up the brown boxes and pour out all the coins, then place them back in, counting them one by one, and snap the top shut.

Skyler builds a Lego Empire State Building, his masterpiece. It is about three feet tall, and he works on it for months. It's so beautiful, mostly done in all black bricks with clear blocks for the top so it appears translucent. He makes an antenna that reaches up to the sky. He gets everything perfect, down to the last detail. It is displayed proudly in the living room and I must touch it every chance I get.

"Mom! Get over here!" Skyler shouts.

I have taken a Lego boy and girl and tried to place them in the Empire State Building model. In doing so, I broke off the antenna and am now standing next to the building, trying not to cry.

"Brittany broke the antenna," Skyler yells to Mom as he points at the broken pieces.

"Why are you messing around with Skyler's Legos? You know how long that took him to build!"

"But I wanted the people to see it and go inside." I look down at the two figures in my hands, a girl with a brown ponytail wearing all pink and a boy with black hair wearing blue.

"If you want to play with Legos then you can build your own set," Mom says.

"But I can't build what he did. I wanted them to live in the Empire State Building. I want them to have a house and be happy."

"Well, then you should know how hard it was for him to build that whole thing! Maybe Sky can help you build something of your own."

Mom leaves and Skyler sees me holding the figures. I stare at the building, admire it, and cry because I'm not able to build one. He knows that I couldn't complete my own Lego set if I tried. I want him to feel sorry for me, sorry enough to help me do the things he can do because he's good at them.

"If I build you a Lego house will you stop messing around with mine?" Skyler asks.

"Yes!" The idea of having my own Lego set that I could play with whenever I wanted fills me with excitement.

Skyler takes out the plastic bins and begins to build my house. I lay down on the blue carpet. The threads are thick and I grab strands and twirl them around my fingers. I stick the two figures I had taken into the carpet so that only their heads are showing.

"Look," I say. "They're safe."

"Safe from what?" Skyler asks as he continues to build the foundation for a house on top of a flat green Lego board.

"They were cold but now they're under the grass."

"Grass isn't blue," Skyler corrects me.

"Well, in your room the grass is blue, and in mine the grass is pink."

"That's just our carpet. It's not grass."

"It can be," I say, removing the Lego people from the carpet. "It's just pretend."

Skyler already has rows of bricks in a square shape inside the green board. It's coming along nicely and I know he's working fast to appease me, his little sister.

"Why don't you let me finish your house and I'll bring it into your room when I'm done?"

"Okay!" I shout, raising my arms with a plastic figure in each hand and running out of the room. I put the Lego figures in my desk drawer and lie down in bed. I love my bed so much. It's a daybed, so I'm told, and it looks like a couch when I'm not sleeping in it. It has white framing and gold balls on the ends. My comforter is paisley flowers done in pastels and the quilted material is fluffy and comfortable. My stuffed animals hang on my closet doors on hooks that Mom got from a home goods store. Each one has their own spot, some I can't even reach because they're up so high, but I put my favorites toward the bottom anyway so I can visit with them frequently. My bookshelf is in the corner of the room with an area for me to sit down next to it. Outside is a view of all New York. I can see the bus stop below where the bus picks us up and takes us to the city on weekends, whenever we want to go.

Life is so comfortable, so nice, so perfectly placed out in front of us. I drift off to sleep and dream of Lego figures. Later, my brother will wake me up and show me the house, how I can take the roof off to safely place my happy Lego people inside, how to be gentle with the pieces this time.

Lego heads tumble in the bin. Lego heads frown and smile. Lego heads are pinched and clicked onto Lego bodies. Arms are folded outward. Hands are twisted prongs. Legs are straightened to slide onto rectangle blocks. He searches for the right Lego face. He searches to find the one he wants, the one that might fit the scene he builds, the one that might represent how he feels. He searches in the bin. He searches. He searches.

Into the Hudson

Mom and I are in the car. I'm wearing my brown-and-white fleece jacket (Mom has the same one, but bigger, the adult version) and I drink my box of Hershey's chocolate milk. We exit the garage of our apartment and drive into the gray daylight. She turns the corner. There is a straightaway looking out at the Hudson River. I'm still groggy from sleep, not a morning child, only soothed by my milk-box whispering, deflating as I drink. My Velcro sneakers don't touch the floor mat. A winter hat sits next to me that I have to put on before I get out of the car. I fan out my hands to admire my *Wizard of Oz* gloves. Each finger is a different character. The Tin Man is my favorite, leathery and gray on my pointer fingers. As we turn the corner, Mom slows down. "Why don't I just drive this car right into the Hudson?" I stop drinking my milk, the box wheezes to a halt and I stare ahead at the river. It looks cold and deep and far away. The trees outside stand still, brown leaves falling and dying as they fall—a story I heard on the playground that I tell myself whenever I see a lone leaf plummet to its death. I don't answer. Mom presses her foot to the pedal and accelerates. We are headed right for it. She keeps going, speeding up, driving straight ahead, moving forward, fast. I ball my fists and shield each character. I imagine floating coats and cold skin, trying to understand what it would be like to die today, to go with my mom into the water and never return. Maybe this is what she wants, for us to be together. Maybe this is the only way I will ever understand what it is to be a mother. On the first day of school, I say "housewife" when the teacher asks what my mom does. "Stay-at-home mom," the teacher replies and marks it down in a big book. My lunch bag is always decorated with stickers. There are always fruits formed into shapes: an orange rind carved into a purse, the grapes are little pennies. If my mom wants to go, that's what we'll do. We'll go together into the Hudson. At the last second she swerves. We turn left, the way to school, continue our morning drop-off where I don't want to leave my mother, don't want to go to school, am afraid to be alone. I frustrate her with my tantrums. I make her angry when she has errands to run and I say I need her to stay with me, just a bit longer, just for a second more. This is the only love that I know in my life. It is warm and it is comfortable.

Papagalos

I am five years old. I am sitting in a plush chair in a fancy restaurant in the Cayman Islands. Papagalos, the restaurant with the parrots. We always come here during our yearly weeklong trip to the Caribbean. We like to take vacations. We live in New York, but it's too cold in the winter, so we head to a warmer climate and come back as tan little faces wrapped in bubbly coats and puff boots.

We rent a car and drive from the airport into town. The drive is my favorite part of the trip: the warm winds blowing from an ocean I only get to see once a year, the way Mom lists off all the exciting excursions we're going to take this time, the promise of fun things to come. I love looking out the window while Dad drives, while Skyler plays video games. We make sure to stop at the local supermarket and stock up on chocolate milk boxes for me, cereal for Skyler, snacks for the hotel room.

A few weeks ago a kid in my class had a birthday party at Gymboree. I wasn't very close with him, but I saw him fall off a chair and crack his head open. Blood got on the mats that I had tumbled across earlier. He wanted to try a somersault from up high. It looked fake, the blood, the slit in his head, and the other kids said they could see his brain. The party ended early and I became anxious. Something stirred inside me that did not go away overnight, with a good night's sleep, with a box of chocolate milk.

Papagalos is known for its plethora of parrots that line the restaurant in glass showcases. Right now they all seem to be squawking at once. The anxious feeling heightens. My parents peruse the expensive menu. Mom orders her French onion soup, and Dad, a hearty cut of meat. My brother is entranced with his Game Boy, already knowing his order, the same thing he always gets, the spicy shrimp. My world is uncertain, though. I think about Ben Gula, his head cracking like an egg, fragile, Humpty Dumpty, no big deal, a hospital visit, stitches, and missing school. What if he doesn't make it? What if he's not okay in the end? And I'm here, in the Cayman Islands with my family, wearing a dress and ordering a side salad. When will these vacations end? What will I be like in the future? How long does it take to grow up?

I feel it in my mind before I see it there, the big bug stuck to the back of my thigh. I know it's there. I can feel its shape. The oval torso, the blackness of its body. Tiny feelers searching for air. My plump little thigh, shaking. I cry silently at the table, but I want it to be dramatic. I want the tension to build for everyone at the table. I think about taking a sip of my water and spilling it in a histrionic fashion.

I think about moving around so the next table can see, the shriek of a woman, the sheer fear it would cause.

The soup is placed in front of Mom. She leans over to me and asks if I'm crying. She knows this is what I do. Kids who cry get taken away, but where do they go? They go elsewhere, and that is where I want to be. Ben Gula was taken away, treated with special care. I turn my face toward her, but do not speak. Then it becomes a scene. Then it becomes the set of one of my many melodramas. I turn my leg toward her and she bats the thing away like crazy. Skyler discards his Game Boy and smashes the bug on the floor with his dress shoe. The bug is dead.

I don't stop crying though. My dad gets angry and says, "Don't ruin the meal because of a bug. It's dead. Didn't you see Skyler kill it? It's over. Get over it!" He cuts into his steak and keeps eating. The birds are crying, carrying on. Skyler watches our waiter sweep away the last of its legs into a dustpan. Dad points to Skyler's shrimp and he continues eating as well.

It is then customary for Mom to escort me away from the family, which is exactly what I want, the whole purpose of this dance. She takes me into the bathroom and lifts up the fluffy tutu of my black evening dress. She washes the spot where the big, fat bug was with cold water. I don't want the ordeal to be over though. No bloodshed, no foul. I want more. I need attention, crave it badly.

We go to the bar so I can sit on an adult stool and feel important. The bartender jokingly asks for an ID, and then gives me a glass of water with a lemon sliver. I pinch the lemon—fleshy, yellow—and plop the seeds into my drink so I can try to suck them out, one by one.

Mom looks upset, as if she has figured me out and yet still doesn't understand me. She tightens my braid and asks, "Why do you do these things?" I start crying again, harder, uncontrollably this time. I am suddenly aware that my mom will die one day, like the bug, like our family trips, and that all of this will end. Like Ben Gula, my mom is not indestructible. She can crack and break, she can choose to ignore me, the way I am, the way I have become. But I need her. I need her to bobby pin my hair and pick out my dresses. I need someone to take me away from the bad scenes, from the hard things, from the things I don't want to see.

I drop down from the stool and hug her leg, my head leaning on her hip.

"I'm scared you're going to die," I say, shyly, afraid that saying it might make it real, might make it happen.

"I'm not going to die for a very long time," she says.

And there we are, the two of us. We play this game for years and years. I do not want my mom to grow old. I do not want to see pain. I do not want to be alone.

Prisoners

When we go out in the city, we all squish into the elevator, layering our bodies and puffy coats, breathing short, excited child breaths, watching each floor light up all the way down. We are always going places in cars, in groups, to the city, to birthday parties, to eat pizza and ice cream cake, to give a present to the kid from class and to take home party favor bags with whistles and parachute-bearing army men. There are always treats, lots of baked goods from the delicatessen, rainbow cookies and almond cookies and the Chinese cookies with big splats of chocolate in the middle.

We are scooped up and taken everywhere with our parents. My brother sits in the front seat of the car and I'm scrunched in the back with Mom. We are never allowed to sit next to each other or we will fight. This is the thought our parents have given us. They don't understand that we like to fight, scream, cry; it's enjoyable for us. It means we are close. It means we are together. There is never a winner, just the separation of our bodies in the car until we get where we are going. Dad smokes cigarettes inside the car and I form a makeshift air mask with the sleeve of my jacket. I pretend I am in a safe, little incubator, like ET, while my brother stares out the windshield. He doesn't mind the smoke, as if he is developing an early taste for things that are bad for him.

Sometimes, the babysitter comes. Renee is our babysitter with the big brown eyes and long brown hair. She understands us and the games we like to play, how we run around the house and time our heartbeats with a toy stethoscope because we want to hear our insides. She lets us build forts on the couch out of big pillows and our large lion stuffed animal. She doesn't get mad when I spill the carton of milk on my head and have to take another bath. She is a teenager, and she encourages us to be children. She likes how I make up stories about the books on my bookshelf, not yet able to read them, too young to understand the words. She helps me make fake pancakes in my Fischer-Price kitchen.

Renee wears sweaters and skirts with sneakers. She takes off her shoes, as instructed, when she steps into the apartment. Sometimes she wears high-waisted pants with a big shirt billowing out. I listen to her because she is beautiful and fun. I act cute and shy around her. I open my eyes big and pout when my parents leave. I pretend I am sad because I know that will make her do things like hold my hand and hug me.

As time goes on, it becomes clear that Renee and my brother are cooler than I am, or could ever be. They speak in double-g language. Their pillow forts never fall down. Renee talks on the phone or reads a Judy Blume book, and

Skyler just wants to play video games and shoot plastic guns. I get demoted to Nerf gun ammo collector.

I don't want to be a kid anymore. I want to be older. I want to be ages twelve and up, like it says on the Lego boxes in my brother's room. I want to understand why older people do and say the things they do and say. I want to win the high score. I want to get all A's. I want to wear sweaters with skirts and sneakers. I look down at my own stupid shirt, the purple velvet one, long sleeves, warm enough for the city weather, but I feel dumb in it, like a child.

Renee stops coming once Skyler is old enough to take care of us both. Skyler ties me to the leg of the pool table with my own green and yellow jump rope and tells me to stay. He doesn't like when I play with his Buzz Lightyear Chrome Edition figurine. I stay tied to the table until I figure out how to untie the knot. I make jelly on crackers in the kitchen, play with my Barbies, and then return to the table leg, retie myself, and wait for his next move. Skyler comes back and lectures me on what it means to be a prisoner.

"If you work hard, you will get one shiny coin a day." He sips from a box of chocolate milk and paces the floor thinking of my next punishment. "You will retrieve my Nerf gun ammunition during the battles, but you must do so in your shackles!"

He returns to his room, forgetting me temporarily. I wait until the little hand moves a bunch of space on the clock on the living room wall, untie myself again, and go into his room to watch him play Mario Kart. I sit on the floor and slowly make my way up to the bed and put my head on his soft, blue pillow. He moves onto the floor so I can get comfortable. We can be together in the same room and not kill each other because he is playing his game and I am watching him. This activity requires me to accept that he is older, better at the game, and that if I sit here and watch quietly, I can be a part of it.

In between levels, my brother asks me if I remember the day Mom left us alone with Dad. He says Dad yelled and Mom cried and he watched it all. He tells me that Dad yelled at him, told my brother it was all his fault, and then went back into our parents' room. He says he stood by the door and waited for my mom to come back for hours. Skyler had watched her walk down the long hallway, to the elevator, then away, gone, not knowing if she would return.

He reminds me that when she came back, she took him to a friend's house, and took me out for a treat. I remember that part. I remember how Mom and I shared Chinese cookies on a walk to the park and she told me, "These are my favorite." I had said, "Me too," because her eyes are hazel and so are mine, something she passed down to me, as I am told. Her hair is dirty blond and blown out so that it bounces and frames her glowing face. She was wearing a patterned sweater and soft jeans and I wore a miniature version of this outfit because I am her daughter and I will grow up to become her. I want to be just like her with her pink cheeks and feathered hair. I want to have a favorite cookie and children who cry for me when I am gone. I want to be missed and know what it is like to miss someone so deeply that it hurts my insides, the ones I can hear on the stethoscope.

My pink room has a view of the Henry Hudson Parkway. I can see the street below and the edges of our white brick building. I can never tell whether it's snowing or if it's just an illusion. I have to look all the way down to see whether the cars are actually caked with snow.

My brother's room has the best view. Out his window, the New York City skyline is a silent stretch of lines and organized shapes. The game on the screen blares, honking, bustling, shooting, swerving. The picture of New York outside is quiet. I drift away into a Mario dreamland of boxy clouds and rainbow roads. The noises of the game do not wake or startle me; the sounds lull me to sleep, peaceful and soothing, like the city in all of its chaos.

Bullfight

Our family takes a plane up and away from everyone we know to spend Thanksgiving in Cancún, Mexico. There is parasailing, relaxing hammocks, and kids' club treasure hunts, which we always win. A giant box of chocolate is delivered to our room with a card that says congratulations in Spanish. Our hotel TV gets Nickelodeon and I watch *Rugrats* for the first time ever. I don't really like it but all the other kids in my second-grade class do and I want to be in the loop.

The same string of photos is taken each year when we come to Cancún. Me in a swimsuit next to a palm tree, me in a hammock, me building a sand castle and giving up halfway because it's too hot.

All I want to do is play with my Barbie doll. I've become obsessed with these skinny women, and tonight, Barbie has a date and needs to get ready. Mom won't let me stay in the hotel room, so I have to come up with reasons to sneak away and go upstairs. A stomachache usually works, but sometimes she wants to accompany me and make sure I'm okay. Telling her I want to change my bathing suit worked once, but the next time she refused.

One morning, Dad takes my brother and I offsite to a water sports place where we rent a boat and go snorkeling. He asks the manager for the best little boat. The boats are meant for two, but fits the three of us perfectly, as I wedge between Dad and Skyler. I wear my favorite leopard bathing suit and Skyler seems somewhat excited to look underwater at colorful fish and maybe see something cool.

The snorkel trip leaves the dock and all the little boats and little families follow the leader. Dad drives us out into the ocean like a flock of birds, following and flying in one direction. The water is so blue and so green. I am nervous to snorkel, since the only time I've ever done it was unsuccessfully in the hotel's lake. Dad made me go in and I knew I wasn't supposed to because it was a lake and not a pool. I knew that this water was for looking at and admiring and not for swimming in. But I went in and he taught me to spit in my mask to make it clear. He told me to rub the saliva into the lens with my thumb and not to rinse it after. He wanted me to see things clearly, as clear as possible. When I saw my first fish, a blue and black angelfish, I splashed in the shallow water and ran out, back to the beach, back to Mom who was waiting with a towel.

The boat sputters and gives out. It comes to a slow in what seems like the middle of the ocean. We are stranded. The other boats have zipped off to continue their adventure. Dad throws a fit with curses and exclamations. No one sees. No one comes. What happens if no one hears his aggravated screams? What happens if we never make it off the boat? Will we swim to safety? What will Mom think? I fear for my own life, the life of my dad, the life of my brother.

I look out at the beautiful Mexican mountains and think of the bullfight Dad took us to the other day. Mom didn't come to that either. The bull ran around the ring, around and around, chasing the toreros with the red blanket and I didn't know why. Everyone was shouting and excited and I didn't understand. I knew that I should be excited. Dad was enthralled. Skyler was happy.

The matador stabbed the bull in the head with a sword. The crowd went wild. I began crying into my shirt and hid that I was sad because I didn't want to ruin anything. Dad cheered and Skyler agreed with him for once. They felt something that I did not. The bull was dead.

The boat is stopped. After a while someone from the water sports shop comes and rescues us. He ties our broken boat to his and we ride back to land. I'm still wearing my life jacket when Dad insists on a refund. Skyler unclicks my jacket and we are safe.

Back at the hotel Mom is glad we are alive. The excursion took three hours longer than she had expected, but it's still daytime, which means time to go downstairs. I open up my Barbie luggage set to play while everyone else gets ready for the pool. The maid seems to have moved it around and things have shifted inside. Barbie's kitchen is in shambles. Her clothes have fallen off hangers in her closet. Shoes are missing and I am upset. Mom nudges me to get my bathing suit on, that we're leaving soon, but I won't move. I continue to dress Barbie for her date in a tight red dress and attempt to restore her living quarters to normal. Mom insists we go down to the pool and I tell her, no. She says I won't be allowed to play with Barbie for the rest of the trip if I don't go now, so I pack the luggage back up to the best of my abilities and stow it away in the mini closet.

Sometimes, things happen for my family like magic. The way watermelon flavored water is waiting for us at the front desk when my parents go to complain about something, or how Skyler and I were the ones who found the treasure first, knowing where to look, having the right guess to get us that huge box of chocolate. But other times the luck is on the other side. Sometimes Dad picks the wrong boat. Sometimes Barbie doesn't get to go on her date. Sometimes we don't apply enough sunscreen, even though we are told to, and we burn in the hot, hot sun, and it hurts.

This is the trip to Mexico when Dad busts his hand open on a glass display at a local mall. He is rushed to the hospital and needs stitches. This is the trip where we can't help ourselves from running around near the pool and Mom reminds us of when she broke her leg, which I don't remember, but I know it to be true. This is the trip where Skyler goes scuba diving and I'm allowed to try it out in the pool. I remember going down each step, letting myself sink deeper, deeper into the depths of the blue pool. This is the trip where I get to take Koko, the class pet, (a monkey stuffed animal) with me, and forget about him until the last day.

We make up for lost time with a string of photos; Koko in a pair of sunglasses next to a palm tree, in the hammock, in the sand with a shovel in his plush little hand.

When I bring him back to school he smells like suntan lotion and there is sand embedded in the fibers of his body. Koko was supposed to go everywhere with me, but there were certain places I couldn't take him. He couldn't go swimming or get wet, he couldn't come on the boat in case he fell out, he couldn't come to the bullfight and watch his brethren die. Most of the time, Koko stayed in the room sitting atop my Barbie luggage, keeping it company, waiting for me to come back, to see what was next.

Square Pizzas

Every Thursday Skyler accompanies me to my ice skating lesson. He's a much more advanced skater than I, as I am only six years old and can barely walk on the ice. I always begin my lessons by clutching onto the rails while the instructor holds up my tiny body. I fumble around on the wall until I find my balance. While I struggle to get through my lesson, Skyler skates along perfectly. His legs stretch out and graze the ice. But regardless of whether I learn a new technique, or even stay on my feet the entire time, I always get pizza from the snack stand after my lesson.

The snack stand at the ice skating rink is old and dilapidated. A health inspector probably should have shut it down long ago, but I love that stand more than anything. I'm impressed by its glowing aura, the orange neon sign, the wafting smells of pizza and hot dogs and nachos. There is a small window for ordering your food and two separate lines, one that reads "Order Here" and the other "Pick Up." The window is too tall for me, so Skyler becomes the designated lookout and shouts when the pizzas are ready. There is a large black marquee over the window that has contrasting white lettering. The snack stand has other things like pretzels, Italian ice, Coca Cola products, etc., but the only thing we are ever interested in is pizza. The pizza isn't ordinary pizza. It's square. It's not Sicilian, though, just square. The edges are always crispy and burnt and there is more cheese than tomato sauce. It comes in a little cardboard box where we pile up our crusts for Mom to eat afterwards.

The hot little pizzas cool down by the time we get to the car and we eat them on the way home. It's warmth to us, the pizza. It may even be love.

"Shouldn't five-year-olds be able to lace up their own skates?" Mom asks. She has on her brown-and-white flannel fleece. It is early November in New York and the autumn chill is slowly turning into winter.

"It's okay," says Jen, my instructor. "I don't mind, really."

Jen kneels down and laces up my brown leather skates. Her blond ponytail sways frantically as I lick my lips at the sight of the snack stand. A little curly-headed girl is eating Italian ices and gives me an evil look while biting down on the wooden stick. I whimper and tug on Mom's fleece, but she just pats my head and assures me I'll get a treat after the lesson.

Skyler watches as I tremble up onto my feet with Jen's help. We walk over from the bench area to the rink and begin the lesson.

"Wanna go get your skates?" Mom asks Skyler.

"Why can't I just play my Game Boy today?" He retaliates.

"But you're so good! You can play your Game Boy on the way home. I want to see you skate!"

"Watch her skate," Skyler says as he hears one of my fearful screams from the ice rink.

"Sky," she groans. "Get your skates."

Skyler laces up his skates. I imagine he hates that the only ones they had left were white, and they aren't even his size. They must feel so pristine, he doesn't want to get them dirty. Even though he ties them up as tight as he can, the leather wobbles around his ankles a bit when he tries to walk around. He is five years older than me, but he is still sort of small. He has dark brown hair, almost as dark and black as the color of his hat and gloves. He wears a big coat over a waffle-printed thermal shirt. His brown eyes stand out and the black pupils look like the little black beads in my Pretty Pretty Princess game. He takes his hands out of his gloves and walks over to Mom.

"Can you at least hold my jacket?" he asks, presenting the jacket to her.

"Keep that thing on!" she screeches. "It's freezing in here. You're not skating without it. You're going to get sick."

"Ok then," Skyler groans. "I just won't skate. That's fine."

His eyes are drawn to the one Pac Man machine that is unoccupied at the time. Mom holds the jacket out in front of him like a children's paper snowflake project, as if she expects him to be elated with it. Skyler reluctantly loops his arms back through their holes and pulls at the collar.

Skyler steps onto the ice. The large arena is illuminated by the daylight from windows on the roof. The ice is white with blue and red lines for hockey players and is scratched up pretty bad. His cheeks, flushed by the cold air, are the color of a faded red Lego brick found at the bottom of an old plastic bin. His small hands plop into each glove as they dangle over his fingers, the ring finger sliding awkwardly in the middle finger's place. He rearranges the black fleece glove so that it is tightly secured, as if he is putting on his armor. Skyler looks for me on the ice. He sees all the skaters, some learning jumps with their instructors and some practicing a routine just by themselves. The afternoon is very popular for lessons and there is rarely free skating allowed.

He finally catches sight of me. There I am, wavering on the ice holding dearly onto Jen. I'm learning how to walk backward on the ice. A skill, Skyler always told me, that he never even used when skating. But he notices that I seem to be better at walking backward than just simply standing up. Harder tasks are sometimes easier for me, and the easy things often seem impossible.

"Over here!" shouts Mom. "Let's see some skating!"

Skyler does a few laps around the rink. He starts out gliding one foot in front of the other, the way he knows ice-skating is supposed to look. An older man zips past him practicing a routine and startles him. He begins to skate a little faster.

Mom motions Skyler over in the stands. He glides over to her.

"What?" He asks Mom.

"Why don't you do some tricks?"

"There's a lot of people on the ice. I don't want to get in anyone's way."

"That's ridiculous. You can practice and do whatever you want. No one is going to bother you."

"Look!" Skyler points. Jen and I skate backward past where they are standing. Jen points at Mom and I wave to her, then stumble, then smile again.

"Come on," Mom says and looks at Skyler. "Show me some tricks."

Skyler steps back onto the ice. His lips are a little chapped from the cold and he pulls up his fleece collar above them. He skates out into the middle of the rink. He balances himself on one foot with his arms out at each side. He catches sight of Mom's smiling face and decides to continue. He does a jump in which he completes a single rotation and lands on the ice a little wobbly. Practicing this jump another four or five times, he becomes more at ease on the ice and less concerned with Mom watching him. He wants to master the jump.

He pushes his left skate forward and the right one back, propelling him forward on the ice. He glides around the rink faster and faster. He knows that the only way he can perfectly complete the jump is if he skates really fast, which will give him enough momentum to turn in a full circle and land perfectly.

Skyler picks up speed. Mom watches from behind the glass, eyes glued on her son.

"Go as fast as you can!" she screams.

The metal on Skyler's ice skates dig into the ice. A sheer mist of frost spews out from the bottom of his skates. He stops and sees Mom standing there watching him, waving her arms around in the air. She looks so happy, but he wants to stop. I am nowhere in sight now and he thinks that my lesson might be over. He wishes that it were over so that he can step off the ice, get into the car, and play his Game Boy on the way home. He is getting tired and begins to feel the cold of the ice rink. He's glad he put his jacket on after all.

"Go as fast as you can!" she shouts again.

Even though he wants to stop, he doesn't want to disappoint Mom. He knows that if he doesn't skate faster, she will just bug him to do it the next time I have my skating lesson. She won't be able to forgive him. She wants to see her son do great things, amazing things, earn accomplishments, win certificates and awards, be the best. Mom wants him to keep going and he knows that it will never stop.

His skates slice into the ice like a meat cleaver at the Riverdale Deli. He feels like an army man parachuting down from the balcony of our apartment, swift and agile. The rink is silent and all he hears is the swishing of his pants as his feet pass one in front of the other in a straight line toward where Mom is standing. He pictures himself on Mario's Rainbow Road floating quickly on the ribbons of color about to reach the finish line. As he reaches his right foot forward, his feet shake because the skates are a size too big, causing the toe pick of his skate to dive into the ice. His small frame smacks right down into the ice and he hits his head, hard.

A crowd forms around him. Skyler rolls over to his side and spits out splotches of blood onto the ice as his lip bleeds, profusely. A large gash on his forehead drips down his eyebrow and on his cheek. Tears well up in his eyes but he doesn't cry.

An attendant carries him out of the rink and lays him on a bench.

"Skyler! Skyler!" Mom runs over toward him, shrieking. "This is all my fault," she says picking up his head and examining his forehead and lip.

"I shouldn't have listened to you," Skyler replies, his eyes beginning to close.

I am standing by the snack stand, completely unaware of the events. My lesson ended a while ago and I am ready for my treat. I stand on my tippy toes and watch the snack man with black curly hair use a big wooden paddle to extract pizza from the oven. I watch him take a round metal slicer and cut the pizza into individual squares.

"I want that one!" I whisper as the man cuts an edge piece, which contains two corners worth of crust and maximum cheese. I know Mom will like all the extra crust.

The man puts the pizza slices under a heat lamp on display for all the customers to look at. My eyes water from looking at the pizza so long and being so close to the heat.

"We have to leave right now," Mom says firmly as she strides by and plucks me away from the snack stand. Skyler stumbles behind, holding an ice pack on his head.

"But what about the square pizzas?" I whine, as I get taken farther and farther away from the snack stand.

"It's my fault," Mom repeats. "It's all my fault."

The three of us walk outside to the parking lot and head for Mom's white Cadillac. I cry as I reach back to the snack stand. Skyler holds up tissues and ice packs to his bloody and bruised face, which makes me cry harder. My brother is a mess and I don't get my pizza. I have no idea what's going on and why. It's so unlike our routine to leave somewhere in a rush, without all the treats, without the things we both want. I wonder if we'll ever even come back. When something horrible happens to a family are they allowed to go back to the places where it happened? Will my brother be okay? Will my mom stop yelling? Will I ever get my square pizza again?

"Why . . . can't I . . . just get . . . pizza?" I cry, hyperventilating.

"We need to get Skyler home," Mom says, wiping her tears with the back of her hand.

I let out a scream. Mom places me in the backseat of the car and buckles my seatbelt. Skyler gets himself into the front and pulls down the mirror. His face is completely black and blue mixed with the red-crusted blood on his eyebrow and the streaks down his face. He wipes up most of the blood, but has to hold the ice pack in place so that his forehead won't swell up.

"How am I going to tell Dad?" Mom is frantic.

Skyler looks out the window with his swollen eyes and sees the large building that we always pass on the way home. We were never really sure what it was for, but on the side of the building is a giant splatter painting that is blue, red, and yellow. Every time we pass it when driving, we always fight over who had painted it. "I painted it!" I would demand. "No, you're too young to paint anything that big, I did it!" Skyler would proclaim. Then Mom would simply turn to both of us and say, "You both did it."

Today, only Skyler sees the painting as we drive by. Mom is too busy rehearsing how to tell Dad about disfiguring their son and I am too upset, still hollering and crying hysterically.

Skyler turns to me in the backseat. I am crying with my head down in my purple puff coat, unable to move my arms because the coat is so big. He tries to offer me his Game Boy, but I won't stop crying. I don't know how to play it yet anyway. I've only watched him press the buttons, the faded purple A's and B's, the little plus sign switch, but I'm not sure how it all works and I'm not interested now. Tears splatter onto the nylon fabric as I breathe heavily, whispering incoherent cries about the pizza I didn't get. Only he can understand.

Escape from the Bottom

We come to Aruba every year for Christmas. We spend fourteen days here, which seems like a lifetime, and it is. Buffet breakfast every morning. Bingo every afternoon by the pool. Hors d'oeuvres every night in the concierge lounge. I love to fill myself up with all these things. I eat strawberry ice cream in a cup, white chocolate swans float in puff pastry boats. I count paper bills from a bingo win, spend them in the game room, win a plush toy from the grab machine, do cartwheels down the hall, out of breath, get back before curfew, set the stuffed animal on the cot, brown blanket over white sheets, line up all the little guys, put them in a row, make them all look nice, count them one by one. These are the winnings, these are the treasures, this is what matters now. Tomorrow there will be more, but never enough.

Mom is excited to lie out on the beach; she wakes up at six to claim lounge chairs, enough for our whole troop, all the families we've made friends with over the years. Dad goes snorkeling and scuba diving, usually with my brother, sometimes with the other dads, and enjoys Clam's Casino or steak with us at night. Skyler likes the arcade room down by the pool and expensive cabanas. It is where all the kids go to exchange coins for moments of joy. Our parents wish he would play in the sand all day like me. I take a shovel and scoop wet sand from near the water and put it in a pail. Then I move it to the jungle gym near our lounge chairs and tiki huts and unpack it into the dry sand. I'm accomplishing something big in my mind. The dry sand needs wet sand and I'm the mechanism that supplies it. The other little kids understand the importance of this. We work all day until we get called for bingo.

I leave the pool early to go upstairs and dry my hair before cocktail hour with all the kids and their parents. I blow dry my hair upside down like in the commercials and then fluff it up as I walk down the long hallway. The older girls tell me I'm pretty as they pet my hair and I eat sugar cookies off a dessert plate. I figure if I can get in with them I can finally get a boy to notice me. All the kids are growing up. When the older kids talk, they gather in circles and discuss plans for the evenings, plans I won't be a part of because I'm too young. They talk about taking turns getting out of control, something about no drinking age and fake IDs, and I figure it's something that happens once you get bored with Beanie Babies and Barbie dolls.

The girls are teenagers now, breasts coming in and bodies fuller, more appealing. I run around in my leopard print one-piece and take a strand of hair out of my ponytail, string it beside my face and pose sexily by the jungle gym, trying to get Jake, a boy I am in love with, to notice me. He is playing Ninja Turtles and wants me to play too. I'm supposed to be April, but I'm Brittany, hand on my hip, waiting for something to happen. Jake hides behind a pillar and another boy lurks around the corner. Jake yells "Splinter's gonna get me!" and the two chase each other in circles. I don't have a role in this game other than to be happy when Jake, as Michelangelo, finally shoots Splinter with a water gun and wins.

When the boys tell me I can't be a Ninja Turtle, I suggest we try kissing and bat my eyelashes like I saw before somewhere. He grabs the other kid and they walk toward the water. I watch them walk away, little boys on the beach in baggy shorts, tiny tan shoulders, I watch them leave me.

I walk over to Mom knowing that she will make a suggestion I don't like, but hoping that this time it will be different and I will be allowed to do whatever I want.

"Can I go to the arcade?" I ask. Mom is in her prime. She's got golden hair that she pulls back with a tie-dye scrunchie. She's surrounded by all of her friends, gossiping in a circle underneath the tiki huts and playing Scrabble, her favorite game. She's winning, but it's close between her and Jake's mom. She'll win though, she always does.

"No, *shayna maidel*. You need to stay outside during the day."

"But I'm bored."

"Just relax. This is vacation." She puts down the word "Jo" and everybody questions it. I know it means "friend" because she told me once when we played alone in our apartment in New York. I was home sick from school and she tried to teach me the game but I didn't understand. She helped me find the words among my row of letters.

"Where's Skyler?" I ask.

"He's with Jodi," she says. Jodi is Janice's daughter. Janice is my mom's best friend. They've known each other forever and we've known their kids forever too, who are no longer really kids now I guess.

"Go find Beth, she's bored too!" Janice chimes in, rearranging her letters, looking for something good. "Pre-teens have it the worst."

I say okay, but I don't find Beth or even try. Instead, I walk down the sidewalk path adjacent to the beach, all the way toward the lighthouse. We used to always walk as a family to the lighthouse every year, but it's too far to go alone. I want to go though, and because it's too far is good enough reason to want to walk somewhere alone. I only make it a few hotels over though and see a group, a kid's club perhaps, racing tiny turtles in rectangular wooden boxes with little colored lanes set up and a finish line. You need two dollars to bet, and I don't have any money, so I watch. The girl in charge lets me pet a baby turtle. I hold it in my hand like an Oreo cookie.

One night, our parents all go to dinner and dancing and Skyler and I get stuck with Gail and Andrew. They're the kids of another family here that we are supposed to be close with but don't like. Our parents put us in a cab and we go to a place that has go-karts and arcade games. This is okay with us, but we wish it were just us. I stick with Skyler and watch him play racing games most of the night. I'm not sure what Gail and Andrew are doing and I don't care. Skyler gets tickets every time he wins a race and I pile them up in my pocketbook, a little black sequined cross-body with a picture of a perfume bottle on the side. It's posh and makes me feel older.

Skyler gives me a few tokens so I can play whatever I want, but I only go to a machine where you put in a coin and get plastic ninjas in a bubble. I get two; one for each of us. His is black and mine is blue. I run back to the racing game and show him. He approves with a nod, but his focus is on the laps and curves and jumps of the game.

I love watching him play. It puts me at peace to stand there and hold all the tickets and feel almost like Mom for a minute; proud for such a great kid. But my love for him is more than that. I'm his sister, his only sister, and I always want to be next to him. He's getting older, though. He's a teenager, and I'm still a kid. We're drifting apart because of our ages and the way the world works. I wish I were older so I could understand more things, kiss a boy, feel a greater love than my little body can handle or fathom.

There's a scene in *The Little Mermaid* where Ariel sings about wanting to be human. She bursts through the water and thrusts herself onto a rock, waves and sea spray splash around her as she declares she wants to be part of their world. This is the freedom I crave. The force that pushes me to escape my childhood and feel what adults are always claiming they'll tell me about when I'm older.

All of a sudden, Andrew rushes out into the rows of games in tears. Gail chases after him. Skyler gets up and yells, "What's going on? Where's he going?"

Gail wouldn't let Andrew ride the go-karts and he threw a fit. When she argued, he refused to settle down and ran outside.

"He wants to walk!" She yells. "He's an idiot!"

Skyler and I look at each other. This is one of those moments where we have nothing else in the world to use except our own intuition. All experiences prior have told us not to do such things, but in that look we agree to forsake all that training and to see what happens when we walk home, back to the hotel, and follow the two kids we hate all the way.

Andrew walks in front as the road slowly turns to a dirt path. Gail, Skyler and I follow in a row behind him. Our hotel is in the distance, probably a few miles away, each window lit up, a golden light like little coins from a video game floating and spinning midair.

"It's only three or four miles, it should take us an hour," Skyler reassures me. "Are you okay?"

I nod and hand him his ninja in a bubble. He smiles and says, "Hold onto it until we get back." I put it in my purse and take mine out, the blue one, opening and closing the pop-top.

"Can you stop that? It's annoying!" Gail yells.

"You're annoying!" Skyler says. "You and your brother are both idiots! Andrew, can we please just take a cab back?"

Andrew continues walking, arms crossed, sniffling and sad.

"It's not my fault!" Gail says. "I can't control him."

I know what Skyler's thinking. He actually thinks it's kind of cool that we're walking late at night back to the hotel because we're definitely not supposed to. And he doesn't really care about Gail or Andrew being annoying. He never pays much attention to them anyway. I don't really care either. As long as I'm with Skyler, I'm not scared. My brother is a black belt, like the ninja. I only got to be a blue belt before I stopped, but he got through all the levels.

We don't tell our parents we walked, but Gail tells hers when she tells on Andrew being a brat and then we get in trouble, but not really, just a stern talking to.

We stay through Christmas. There is Santa on the beach giving out presents. There is dinner and dancing on New Year's Eve in my black sequin dress until I tire myself out on the dance floor before midnight. There is a jet ski crash with some of our parents' friends' kids where two of the boys actually get hurt. Everyone is skeptical of the water sports for the rest of the trip, but I'm too young for any of that stuff.

I wake up one morning violently ill. Coughing, snotting, crying. The only clinic is a fifteen-minute cab ride away, which my mom accompanies me to and I lay my head in her lap the whole way. The waiting room resembles what I imagine a third world country would look like. It reminds me of when Skyler plays Rampage and lands on a world tour in a distant city with dusty streets and run-down buildings. Sick kids cover the chairs and floors with red eyes and missing limbs, runny noses and bleeding scabs. I huddle into my mom for protection and she tells me to not to breathe or touch anything.

A small girl is coughing into the air, mouth wide open, and her mother is rocking her baby brother in her arms. The small girl dances around the waiting room until she spins herself dizzy. She then proceeds to vomit on my mom's foot. My mom screams and we run into the parking lot, get in our cab that's waiting, and leave without seeing the doctor.

A few hours later, a doctor comes up the hotel room and listens to my chest as I cough. I'm in my pajamas, which is weird because it's the middle of the day and everyone else is at the beach. "She threw up right on my foot!" my mom tells the doctor who speaks little English and tends to me. "Thank you for coming" my dad says in his polo shirt and bathing suit bottoms. My brother must be with the other kids, out having fun, or being bored, either way they're all together and I'm up here sick in bed. I wonder why I got sick and no one else did. The doctor diagnoses me with a chest infection and I get a bottle of pink liquid to drink from three times a day.

My mom gives me an early Hanukkah present: a drawing set that comes in wooden briefcase. I draw our entire family and cut out the characters so they can move around the room. I also make various outfits for the figures that fold on and off as needed for different occasions. In their swimwear I line them up along the terrace window and face them toward the beach. When I'm done playing I stack them like a little deck and put them into the briefcase so the family can stay together. My mom tells me to go downstairs and lie on a chair with my mouth open to the sun so it will kill the bacteria from the infection. She tells me to put lemons in my hair to make it more blond. In two days, my infection has cleared and I'm a much blonder preteen girl on the beach with nothing to do again.

Our parents allow us to go out again with the rest of the kids. Tonight it's me, Skyler, Beth, Jodi, Andrew, Gail, Jake, and David going out for a pizza dinner. I'm beyond nervous. I don't know what's gotten into me. A few days ago I was playing bingo in a towel with my hair all frizzed with all the other little kids, but now it's just embarrassing.

Tonight I'm sitting here at the pizza place and Jodi is flirting with Skyler. He's playing video games in the corner and she's twirling her hair and smiling. She has beautiful long, black hair that lies straight and flat on her back, almost to her butt. Her eyes are green and she's thin with a Jewish nose, but she makes it look good. She's grown into it. I note her posture, the languid pose of interest yet distant configuration of desire in her eyes. This is the shape of wanting someone, of being attracted, attached, of growing up and feeling something called love or being in love, or wanting to be in love.

David asks me what I want to drink and I try to think of the mature choice and say, water. Water is sophisticated. "You're going to have pizza and water?" Jake taunts. "Don't you like soda or something?" "They have Pepsi," David says. His deep brown eyes and tanned face brood in the pizza parlor. I am still a kid and all I can say is, no. So now I've lied. I'm a little girl who hates soda. This is how it has to be from now on I guess—a life without soda, a life of lies.

The pizza comes and it's good, but it gets soggy with water and I wish I had a Pepsi. Skyler sits down and the whole gang eats their pizzas. Skyler sees that I don't have soda and he looks confused. "Don't you want a Pepsi?" He asks. I shake my head and stare down at the little glowing triangles on my plate. I can tell he knows that something is wrong here, all mixed up, but he doesn't know what and doesn't bother asking.

Jake starts talking about the beginning of the world and Adam and Eve and all that. My brother and I were raised Jewish, but only went to temple for our cousins' bar and bat mitzvahs, so we're not sure what we believe. We know what latkes are and how to chant the Hanukkah prayer, but we're not sure how the whole world began. Skyler had his bar mitzvah on top of Masada last summer in Israel, but most of the time I was just really hot and tired and didn't understand the meaning behind anything. My mom kept saying "Skyler is becoming a man!" but I thought that was something that would happen when he was forty or so. I didn't get how a thirteen-year-old could possibly be considered an adult. Skyler still plays video games and while he always wins, he didn't seem any more grown up than before. Or maybe he was changing, but as a kid I couldn't see it.

"Adam and Eve were the tallest humans in the world and God had to fold them up into boxes every night so they could sleep," Jake preaches.

"That doesn't make any sense!" Gail says. "They were normal people like us. Normal sized and everything."

"No!" Jake insists. "They were so big! And when Eve ate the apple that's when He shrunk everyone else after to normal size."

"That's so ridiculous. Your brother is an idiot, David," Gail says, trying to get David on her side. Jodi and Beth laugh and then have a minor moment of disgust for finding Gail funny. I realize what's going on here. It seems that Jodi has temporarily given up on Skyler, Beth has developed a taste for older men as well, and Gail has a crush too. Everyone likes David.

Andrew, Jake, Beth and I are sent home by our elders. Beth is upset because there is supposed to be something more for her, something she's missing out on by taking a cab home and having our parents pay the fare when we arrive.

Sleepy-eyed Andrew is escorted to his room by his mom. We've all forgotten about the mishaps of yesterday. Every night in Aruba brings about a new adventure for the kids who are getting older, a new disappointment for the preteens, a new toy from the grab machine for me. My dad is too tired to come with me to the game room and my mom wants to watch a movie upstairs, so somehow Jake and I are allowed to go together to the arcade room. The arcade closes at midnight and it's only ten o'clock.

Jake and I race there and I momentarily lapse on my desires for a boy. Jake is the boy and I am the girl. I'm not supposed to win here. I'm supposed to lag behind and pretend I'm tired, wait for him to slow down so I can catch up. Then he can let me win, or beat me and I can congratulate him with loving eyes. But for me it is all about winning, getting there before he can, touching the white door to the arcade and screaming *I win* and making him feel insignificant and slight. "I can't run in my dress shoes!" Jake proclaims.

We walk inside the game room and both become lost in the crowd. There is a pool tournament happening and Jake is an ace at pool. My dad taught me how to play on one of the first nights we were here this year. He showed me how to correctly hold the cue stick and how to best angle the shots. I picked it up pretty quickly, mostly because it is a game that requires a quiet skill, an inside voice, the perfect amount of silent anxiety I am accustomed to. I assume Jake has succumbed to the depths of the pool table and I make my way over to the change machine for tokens.

I change a five-dollar bill, which is a lot of dough in kid money, and I attempt to play a racing game, Cruisin' USA. Skyler always plays this one. I know which vehicle to pick, and to drive automatic because it's easier, even though he always drives manual, but I can't quite grasp the mechanics of the game and I end up in eighth place. I crash into walls and my car explodes, rebuilds itself in technological wonder, and then I land it in a body of water. The big-breasted, bikini-clad animated girls jump around at the finish line where a neon green car is receiving its trophy.

The game room has lost its awe. The walls seem darker. The crowd is different. My brother is not here. Jake isn't actually playing pool, he's just watching an older kid play, a teenager. It seems that's all we'll ever be good at, watching the older kids play while we wait our turn, waiting to grow up and get on with our lives. I walk over to the grab machine and a father and daughter are playing. The girl is about five in a fluffy cupcake dress and hair barrettes strewn about her blond head. She has her eye on a dog with its tongue sticking out of its mouth. The father drops the crane. It lowers into the mass of stuffed bears and turtles and dogs. Colored heads and fuzzy bodies. He clasps a neck and grips it tight. The crane ascends. The claw is filled with a new friend. It's made its escape from the bottom.

She's excited when her father lands the right coordinates and a puppy plops into the prize box. She lifts the lid and hugs it to her chest, and then turns again to good old Dad wanting another friend from the machine. The dad slides in another set of coins and the game lights up again. The red bulbs lining the machine flash to carnival music.

The game depresses me now. There's no excitement anymore; it all feels wrong. Animal heads and legs and butts poke out. I don't see any I would want to put on the cot next to the others. I shouldn't even have stuffed animals anymore anyway. I'm too old. The grab machine is for ages five and under, and I'm eight, a pre-teen, purposeless in a sea of crazy arcade kids wondering where my older sibling is. What is happening out there without us? Is this why Beth is so sad when Janice tells her she can't stay out past eleven? What do they do so late and why can't I go?

I leave the arcade room even though Jake and I are supposed to go back to our rooms together. I question the idea that Jake and I would want to leave a place at the same time. He's fine with how things are. He doesn't care about what happens after dark. He just wants to run and play and be loud and get dirty and be a little shit. All his appeal is gone for me. I think about David on the way back to the lobby and have a moment by a tall palm tree. I stand against it and close my eyes, think about him, his brown eyes and the way he laughs, shy at first but then bursting out. It's dark outside and I wonder where he is now, what he's doing. I hope he's not talking to Gail or Jodi. Maybe he secretly loves me and is afraid because I'm so young. Maybe if I wait until next year, maybe the year after, he'll feel better about it and we can be together, whatever that means.

The lobby is still crowded. There are always people coming and going, entering and exiting. I see a couple getting out of a cab and returning to the hotel. The woman is dressed in a long red dress and the man is in a suit and tie. Her hair is up in a swirl and he grabs her hand and whisks her away into the depths of the hotel. This is what romance looks like. This is something I want.

After New Year's, most people leave, but we're still here. We'll leave in a few days, not sure how many. I don't keep track of time, but I can feel it coming soon, just like I feel I'm not supposed to be in that arcade room anymore. I wonder if my parents are sleeping. I hope they're not mad that I came back alone, but maybe it's a good thing to get in trouble once in a while. David might like that about me.

I go up in the elevator and get off at my floor. I try to sneak by the concierge lady but she sees me and offers me a cookie. It's a sugar cookie, my favorite, with rainbow sprinkles. She's writing in her datebook and smiling at the nothingness of the hour. I look out a window and all I see is the ocean, the waves rolling into one another, a blackness that obscures the room. Out there is where my brother is and the rest of the older kids too. They are doing things and saying things and having fun and getting in trouble and being together and learning what it means to be an adult.

I can't tell what's out there in the night, but I can see it's dark.

"Where is he?" Mom whisper-yells into the dark of our hotel room. My cot is in the corner next to my brother's bed, which is next to my parent's bed. Dad is sitting at the table in the corner at the foot of my bed. They think I'm asleep, but I've positioned one of my stuffed animals under my chin so I can squint my eyes and see underneath its floppy ear. "It's two in the morning, and he's not back yet. What could he possibly be doing out so late?" Dad gets an idea to check the hotel television channel where guests can see what's been charged to the room. There are multiple charges at the hotel pool bar for various alcoholic drinks. They don't seem to believe it to be true though. Mom suggests that someone took the room key and charged all this stuff. Dad doesn't really respond. He opens the terrace door and lights a cigarette.

There is a banging on the door. My dad stumbles up in his pajamas. My brother is unconscious on the hallway floor in different clothing than he was in before. Two boys run toward the elevator.

I don't know what it means or why he is face down on the carpet in someone else's clothes. There's nothing I can do but watch.

I sit up in my cot. Mom and Dad carry Skyler to his bed in the middle of the room. His face is toward the wall on the other side so I can't see if he's alive.

"Go to sleep," Mom insists. "He just needs to sleep it off. He'll be fine."

There's a rumbling sound and Skyler throws up all over the bed. Dad carries him into the bathroom. "Fuck," he says, but he's not mad. Mom tears the sheets from the bed and throws them out the door into the hallway. Dad covers the bathroom floor in towels and lays my brother down next to the toilet. They're not angry. They're mechanical. I cry because I've never seen someone like this.

In the middle of the night I wake up and have to use the bathroom. I forget about the whole ordeal in my slumberous state and walk all the way to the bathroom door only to find Skyler sleeping using a towel as a pillow. I walk back over to my parent's bed and try to wake up Mom. She's fast asleep though.

"Don't wake her up," Dad says, looking at me as I rub Mom's arm.

"I have to pee."

"So go. He won't wake up for a while. I've already gone twice, it's fine."

I stand there in the hotel room. I don't want to pee in front of a boy, let alone my brother. What if he wakes up and sees me and wonders what I'm doing in there while he's in there? Does he even know where he is? Dad sees this isn't going to happen and he puts on his pants and tells me to wait by the door.

The lobby is quiet. I've never seen it like this before but it makes me feel at peace. To know that this is what happens here late at night, to see something I'm not supposed to see, the early morning shift of the hotel and how calm it is. It's comforting that at some point the craziness stops and the hotel takes a deep breath. Dad holds my hand all the way from the elevator to the restrooms and nudges me into the women's room. I'm hesitant though, because when I'm done and we go back upstairs, I'm not sure what will happen next. I don't know if there will ever be calm again. My brother is growing up and I'm not, or maybe I am. Maybe growing up is finding calm in the storm, and if so, I've found it here in the lobby at dawn. My dad in his pajamas, me in mine as well, both of us momentarily enjoying the truce in a battle that is about to take place for the rest of our lives.

The next morning, Mom is back at the lounge chairs playing Scrabble. Dad is out scuba diving with Janice's husband, getting in his last dive before we get on a plane. The rest of the adults are sunning and not wondering where their kids are at the moment. This is when the vacation turns everyone selfish and they want to get what they truly need before they leave. For me this means going to bet on the turtles. This also means I will have to ask my mom for permission.

I approach the tiki hut and wait my turn to speak. Mom is always so presentable. She keeps a bottle of Lancôme liquid blush in her purse to reapply whenever she wants to look more radiant. She slathers it on mine and Skyler's faces after a vacation like this and says it will make our tans stand out.

The moms are talking about what happened last night. Beth sits alongside Janice and helps her pick out letters. "Apparently Gail threw up in the cab!" Beth participates in the conversation. Gail's mom is nowhere to be found to validate or negate this. "That's terrible," Janice agrees in disgust. I wonder about David and if he had any part of this. I think about Jake again and realize maybe he's more my speed. He's back to shoveling sand underneath the jungle gym. He wipes a black tuft of hair out of his face, getting sand all through it in the process and I fall in love again.

"What happened to Skyler?" Jake's mom asks, curious but trying not to be intrusive, but she is anyway.

"He's getting his punishment," my mom says flatly and lays down a word that is impressive, but not winning her the game anytime soon.

"Jodi is punished too," Janice says. "She's up in the room and not coming out until we go back to New York."

I decide it's now or never on the turtles.

"Mom, can I have two dollars to bet on the turtle race?"

"Let's all go," she says, and I rejoice.

My little feet are hot on the pavement but I refused to wear sandals for some reason. Mom pulls them out of her purse and they land on the ground with a slap. I slide my feet into them and feel safe, protected, like a kid, and it's not so bad. I pick the turtle in the purple lane and it loses to the one in the yellow lane, the one Beth picks. She chooses a bottle of bubbles from the prize chest and lets me take turns blowing bubbles with her the whole walk back.

"You're my jo," I say. But Beth doesn't know what I mean and pretends not to hear.

Skyler eats Corn Pops out of a box underneath the tiki hut. His sunglasses are on and the older kids gather around, asking him questions in awe of his drunken feat. This is the first time my brother has ever really gotten in trouble. He doesn't look sorry. He looks out of it. I'm happy to see him not on the bathroom floor. I'm happy to see him up again.

"I'm so upset with him . . . I just don't know what I'll do," Mom says as we walk by. I can tell she wants to ignore him. She doesn't want to deal with the real problem.

Now I understand why my mom suggested that we all go together to see the turtles. She was losing her Scrabble game and all control that comes with that victory. But for me, the turtle race wasn't about winning, it was about getting away. Even though we are all powerless to the outcome of the race and I'm just a kid betting on turtles, we've gotten away from the tight grasp of the rest of our lives, the claw that digs for our heads and bodies, the promise of a prize, the thrill of a win. In this moment on this vacation, Mom can gain back some power; at least one of her children is still a child.

She hurries me toward the towel stand where a couple sells jewelry. They are a husband and wife who live on a boat and travel the world with their two sons. Blond-haired, shirtless boys with shark tooth necklaces and baked little bodies. Mom says I can get something if I want. I've waited the whole trip for her to say those words. All I want is new jewelry to add to my collection. I'll wear it for a month straight and then forget about it forever.

The wife points me toward a pile of necklaces with clay wizard men charms that hold colored crystals in their lap. She says they each have different meanings, depending on the color. Blue is for earth energy. Yellow is for the mind. Green is for nature. Red is for love. Mom says to pick one. I choose yellow. "Yellow will help you in school!" Mom beams. "Yes," the traveling jewelry lady agrees, "rub the crystal during your tests and it will help you focus." They both smile.

I put the souvenir around my neck. I know it looks childish, the wizard in a hat and the crystal, but when the kids in my class ask where I got the necklace, I tell them "in Aruba" and they marvel in awe, like I've done something great, been somewhere cool, farther than they've been and perhaps further than they'll ever go.

Mario Saves the Princess

Pancakes. A stack. There were always too many. Syrup spilling over. Breakfast soup. River of syrup. Too many pancakes. Too much for our little stomachs. The river was dangerous. The river was excess. Mario floats on a pancake. Mario must save the princess. Don't stand in the booth. Don't sit on your knees. Sit on your tush. Eat with your fork. Mario mush. Princess is a knob of butter. Princess is a straw wrapper. Princess is an ice cube floating in the syrup river melting on the pancake mush. Do you want a piece of bacon? Do you want chocolate milk? Do you want to save the princess? My eyes are bigger than my stomach. My little stomach. My little belly. The big stack. The tall stack. Are you going to save the princess? The side plate is an island. Bowser is a saltshaker. Bowser is a pepper grinder. Bowser is a spoon that scoops her up. No one is mad. No one yells. Mario wins. The pancake tower falls. We never finish the stack. The princess is safe. Mario always wins her back.

My brother invents a prototype for a perpetual motion machine. He meets with his ninth grade science teacher once a week to test out his design and go over new findings. I don't understand how it works, but it involves miniature magnets that are supposed to represent bigger, massive ones and something about them turning endlessly once set in motion. He keeps the machine in his room on his desk. When he's not there, I hold the magnets in my hands, flip them over and feel the whoosh of energy, like trying to pull up weeds from the ground at recess, the dirt clinging to the weed, the weed clinging to the dirt.

When I am left home alone I go through everyone's things. I start with my dad because his stuff is all laid out. The Grateful Dead albums lined up on the windowsill in my parents' room in New York City. I am eight and this is very interesting to me. I am a detective and I am trying to figure my family out without them knowing. I open each one, take out the CD and examine it, then place it back into the correct holder, place the cover back over it. I turn on the computer and type something in Wingdings font, something only I will be able to understand, then erase it, X out, and shut it off. Next I move to Mom's jewelry box, the blue and white one where the second drawer is stuck. I open it and take every piece out, lay it on the floor: the pendants of my brother and I as jeweled children on a thin chain necklace, rings that don't fit me, her heart-shaped diamond engagement ring that does fit me that I wear for the duration of the plundering (and I know to put it on my left ring finger because that finger's vein leads to my heart), the pearl necklaces that aren't quite white, white but are more opalescent or beige, some beaded bracelets from Aruba that I have discarded or neglected (the one with the star I reconsider to make a comeback but then realize this would hint to Mom I'd been through her things), and last the Hebrew charms that I can't read but I am told they mean "life" (the symbol resembling a kitchen table). In my mind I understand this; life happens at the kitchen table because families are supposed to talk about their day at dinner. My family doesn't do this. Skyler and I often climb and jump off the kitchen table when no one is around and this once resulted in the scar that still resides on my forehead.

Then it is off to Skyler's room. His is the hardest to infiltrate because I know he can tell exactly where I've been. Even if I try my hardest, I cannot outsmart his genius. In his room I practice the art of going unnoticed. I hover over his miniature car set and scan each row of painted bodies. I touch his blue bedspread and feel the fluffy quilted material under my hands. I spy the chrome edition Buzz Lightyear figurine from *Toy Story* that he never lets me play with. I don't dare touch this one, as my fingerprints would remain on the silver wings, the clear helmet, the gold buttons on his chest. The shelves of *National Geographic* magazines, *Where's Waldo* books, encyclopedias. Bean bag chair. White desk with the Apple logo sticker peeled halfway off that I think I stuck there but I didn't. Series of ballpoint and fine tip pens. Small set of paint and brushes. The perpetual motion machine. The prototype sits on his desk and I'm not supposed to touch it without his permission or supervision. In its stationary state I wonder where all the energy is. What would happen if it actually worked? Could he really save the world? I can't help myself and I thumb the magnets hoping to feel a surge, a rush of something I don't understand.

He told me once about doomsday, how the world will stop spinning, suddenly, without warning. He said he knew when it would happen and I believed him. I trusted him to fix it, to prevent it, to know what was wrong with the world and how to stop it from ending. He becomes my hero before I become the damsel in distress. He is the only one who can save me. He is the only one who knows how.

WINNER WINNER. In big letters it glows on the screen. A floating trophy. Two children in the blue bedroom. New to the area. We don't know the rest of the kids. We play alone on Saturdays with a bin of Legos. I organize faces and bodies. He builds cities. We go out to dinner with our parents. I have a kid's meal. He has an adult meal. We feel smaller than the other kids. We are smaller but we have more things. Our toys took up so many boxes when we moved. The other kids should be so lucky to get to come over and play. A house with a loft. The loft is for all our toys. The Super Nintendo fits nice and snug above the TV set. The cords are tucked behind the entertainment center so we don't see its inner workings. We sit on the carpet and enter the digital world where we belong. I ask you to use your magic feather to jump into the splishy splashy pools. You hop in and I am amazed by the possibilities of this game. I am amazed by you and all the things we have here in this house. Every drawer is filled, all the space is for us, it is ours, you are winning the game and I am watching you all this time.

You are getting older and I feel like I won't. I feel like I will never be your age. You are in high school and I am in elementary school. The Nintendo 64 stays in your room because you are older. I watch you play Starfox. I watch you play Golden Eye. But I like Mario Kart the best. You let me play and teach me all the tricks, the jumps, the way to shoot shells, the way to hop on turns, the boost. I am learning how to be as good as you. Someday I will beat my opponents, someday I will get the glowing, gold trophy and it will matter every single time I do. It will matter because we are the best. Mom still needs to adjust our uniforms for prep school. The khaki pants are too long, the polo shirts are too baggy. She tells people she has to force us to eat ice cream. So many times I threw away cups filled with ice cream because I wasn't hungry, my little stomach, but she wanted us to have the treat. Vanilla ice cream in a cup. She wanted us to have the little vanilla cups.

Dad picked me up from the airport only a few hours before. I was coming home from Chicago. From some bad trip in Chicago. I still had trains and lost love on my mind when the call woke me up. I dropped to the floor and prayed like a hopeless person. The way Dad didn't even quiet Mom when she screamed.

You looked cool, like you always do. You had your shades on, your cargo pants, your black backpack, fully loaded on painkillers, and your gun in the front compartment. If the zipper was loose, if the bag fell, if you wanted me to know, I could have seen the silver barrel shining through the knitted mesh.

Treasure chest. Lego set. Oxys hidden inside. Lego click. Pirates and wenches. Lego palm trees. Oxy set. A Lego hand reaches out, pronged and cupped, toward land, toward the treasure chest, toward what you've hidden.

I felt like I didn't have a brother. I knew I did, but it didn't feel that way. You were a memory, a sunny day on the swings across the street from our old building, a great vacation, a nice time. I looked at pictures and thought *that must have been nice*. Years are dated on the back, 1990, 1992, 1995, 1997, like high scores, going up.

You slept on the couch until morning, until a cop came to the door and asked for you. He searched your bags and found the gun. It's like we didn't have parents, it's like we didn't have anyone telling us what to do, no one to say what's right or wrong. When you lean over the balcony to smoke, they didn't question why or how, but they repeated, "Look what you're doing to your sister" like a glitch in the game.

Years later back in Chicago, I drink beer at a party. I'm in a makeshift cat costume and I lean up against the wall. Everyone is eating chips out of colored bins decorated for Halloween. My best friend is dressed as a witch and her hair lights up blue and green. Someone I don't know walks over and asks me where I'm from. "Somewhere else." The president of Zeta Beta Tau is here, my college hookup, and he invites me back to his place to play Kart. I accept and he is sure he will beat me, but surely he can't. In my cat ears and tight, black dress, I sit on the floor and choose Toad as my character. I hop over the wall at Wario Stadium and he has no chance. He can't catch up and I win. He is frustrated, but still wants me to spend the night. When he asks, I say sure because I don't want to be alone. I leave my controller on the hardwood floor and shut off the game. The screen goes black. Mario Land goes to sleep. Somewhere out there, Mario saves the princess in another player's game. In a simultaneous universe of electricity there are trophies and stars and Bowser is big and Mario is small and the Princess kisses him when he wins. Her face, the crown, her pink dress, all of it lighting up dark rooms, glowing on other screens.

Apples to Oranges

I had to miss the last week of summer camp because we were moving to Florida. My camp counselor carried me to the infirmary (as I frequently complained of mosquito bites) and as the nurse applied the cream that I would immediately wipe off upon exiting, I thought I might actually miss New York. We walked back to the cabin, and my counselor's boyfriend who also worked at the camp held my hands and picked me up on the count of three. "One . . . Two . . . Three!" and up I went. I had made my mark there. I was going to be missed.

I asked Mom to take me to the park with the zip line on the way home, one last time. New York, with its rolling landscape, green parks in the summer and snowy streets in the winter. Tall buildings and trees, our apartment just outside the city, our school, our friends, Dad's side of the family, our whole lives up until then. We were giving all of that up. We were moving and moving on.

Skyler was on a teen tour and came back home to a boxed-up apartment with no time to acclimate. The next day we were in Florida searching for another place to live. He blamed our parents for moving us so quickly like that, not letting us grieve our losses. There were things we had that disappeared, like when I left a Happy Meal toy in the jungle gym in Aruba and it was gone forever, or when he brought his action figure to a gymnastics birthday party and it got lost in the foam pit. In Mom and Dad's defense, they thought it would shield us from having to say goodbye, from feeling too sad. Maybe now that's why we ruin all our goodbyes. I don't think it's that change scares us, but we learned early on that moving forward meant not looking back.

We lived at the Westin hotel in Ft. Lauderdale from July-August in '98. I was ten and Skyler was almost fifteen. We stayed at the hotel all summer. Waking up every morning and getting a free bagel from the concierge, watching *Bug Juice* on the big TV, getting dressed and interviewing at different elementary schools for me and high schools for Skyler. Then came looking at houses all afternoon.

We played a game on those many house tours; who could escape the house having stolen something? While Mom and Dad talked prices with the realtor, we scouted the home for decorative fruit that fit in the palm of our hands, only to be revealed later in the hotel room. One of us always pretended to listen in on the housing conversation. We'd stand behind our parents, tiny versions of the serious, soon-to-be homeowners. We wanted things too, we had demands. We required a pool for swimming, a big loft for playing Legos, and separate bedrooms with not too much distance between them.

Potted plants made good targets for stealing. Usually fake, they allowed us to pluck tiny leaves, flowers. Once a purple orchid that I kept in a playing card box until I was twenty-one. Once, a bamboo napkin holder made its way to my back pocket during a routine showing. When we arrived back at the hotel, we spilled the contents of a day's work out on the floor in front of the TV. *Zorro* glowed on the screen above us; the masked hero, Don Diego de la Vega, whipped through foreign cities in black and white. My brother pretended he was Zorro, wielding a balloon sword we got from Dave & Buster's, protecting me from danger in our hotel room. Pillows were boulders, the bed was a giant cliff, the blanket was a storm, and we always escaped just in time. I remember one night Skyler gave me a purple orchid. "For your troubles," my brother said, and handed it to me the way Zorro handed flowers and gifts to his lovers.

Our parents never found anything we took. It was a crime so harmless, it was like it never happened. And we got bored of it eventually. Maybe we wanted our own things in our own home. Maybe we were tired of all the other houses.

Dad was commuting back and forth to New York during the week, Monday to Thursday evening. He did this for about two years even after we moved. Mom let me sit in the backseat when she drove to the airport at night to pick him up. I stayed up to see them kiss hello when he got into the car, but then I'd fall asleep on the ride back. This was when they still missed each other, whether it was because the chaos of watching after two children got out of hand, or because of actual, real love. It didn't matter to me. I just wanted to see them together. I liked wearing my pajamas in the car and listening to the radio. I liked when he got in the car and I could smell his cologne on him, pungent and manly, entering the car and sitting up front next to Mom.

Our daily activities became mundane. Florida was hot, a kind of hot we've never known. But it rained a lot that summer, so there weren't many "nice" days to go out and play, not that we are even the type to go out and play. Our hotel had a pool, but we never used it. The pool was extremely small, a square, no slides, no hot tub, nothing. A few weeks before we finally bought our house in Boca Raton, there was finally a "nice" day and my mom insisted we go to the pool for a few hours.

Mom sat on a lounge chair and read the paper while my brother and I splashed around the too-cold pool. In the hotel gift shop, Skyler had somehow swindled my mom to purchase us a pair of water guns. This was awesome, and horrible. Everyone liked shooting them, but no one liked being shot. It hurt, as these were cheap water guns with sharp pieces of plastic coming out from all ends, they didn't work properly, only stayed filled for thirty seconds or so, but it was our entertainment.

Any time I got shot, I would wail and throw my hands in the air, pretending to drown, and my brother would be forced to come scoop me up and see that I was okay. Then, with him just where I wanted him, I would gulp up a big sip of pool water in my mouth and then sit up and let him have it, spitting it right in his face. He would push me off of him and throw me back into the water in disgust, where I would once again pretend to drown and the cycle would repeat itself. "I'm really drowning now!" I'd say, head bobbing out of the water and my arms flailing, going from floating to drowning instantaneously.

Mom, Skyler and I were the only people at the pool, and when we got too noisy, she looked up from her paper to scold us. Maybe she was still stressed out from being in the in-between of living situations. We had looked at so many houses in such a short period of time. Maybe she was feeling despair that Dad was away and couldn't help out as much as she needed him to. Or maybe it was just a bad day. She felt we had gone too far and as I latched onto my brother in the deep end and spit water into his face, Mom told us to swim over to the edge. She grabbed the water guns from us, my bright pink gun and Skyler's neon orange gun, and threw them down on the ground. Mine broke instantly, but Skyler's only had a crack down the handle. I grasped the edge of the pool wall and began crying as Skyler screamed "Mom, stop! We're just playing!"

"No, look how upset you're making each other!" She yelled back at us.

"No! Mom!" He screamed back as she lifted up her foot and stomped on his orange gun, breaking it into pieces. The plastic tore into her foot, and she hobbled back to her chair trailing drops of blood on the cement. Neon orange shards were everywhere, scattered among pool water and blood, like a children's crime scene.

A maid passing by saw Mom bleeding and ran to get her help. She went inside to get cleaned off and bandaged. I knew how mad Skyler was, and while normally I would have gotten upset about Mom getting hurt, my fear turned into rage and I understood his anger. He got out of the pool, grabbed his towel, and headed upstairs. We never went to the pool again after that. Mom later apologized for breaking the guns, and offered to buy us new ones, but we didn't want them. We soon moved out of the hotel and into a real house, with a big pool, one we never really swam in for the nine years we lived there.

I remember holding onto the edge of the pool and seeing all that broken plastic. It was getting dark outside, probably going to rain soon, another predictable Florida day of weather. I got out of the pool and picked up one of the solid pieces of my brother's orange gun and tried to piece it back together. It was too hard. I left all the pieces on the ground, broken and brightly colored.

The Transportation Center

We are on the monorail from EPCOT to the Transportation and Ticket Center. When I was little, we used to wait so I could ride in the front car with the conductor. I always wanted to do this, but if the line was too long, we took whatever we could get and rode in another car.

I know all the stops. If you're riding from Magic Kingdom, you'll stop at the Grand Floridian, then the Polynesian. If you're coming from the Transportation and Ticket Center (TTC), you'll stop at the Contemporary and then off to Magic Kingdom. From EPCOT, you only make one stop, but today it's taking longer than I thought it would. I'm looking out the window. Skyler is taking his medication and Mom is watching him. I count each pill as she hands it to him. No one else on board seems to notice this transaction. No one else can see that we are doped up on Disney magic.

Below, there are two men walking on Disney grass. Two employees who make sure the place gets taken care of, that everything works and flows in proper Disney fashion. We pass over them and move into more parking lots. Hundreds of cars, trailers, buses, some adorned with Disney bumper stickers, some with kids filing out wearing matching T-shirts for a field trip, some families making their way into the park. I want to look out this window forever. There's nothing better than warm sun coming through the glass.

I'm home from college for winter break and we're all in sweaters. We come for a day trip this time, hitting up a few of the parks during the day and then driving back home at night. Every time my brother goes to the bathroom I think he's using. Every time he closes his eyes I think he's nodding out. Every time he laughs at something I say, I wonder if it's funny because he's as high as a Georgia pine and he thinks neither Mom nor I can tell.

Yet it's one of the best days of my life. Sitting here on the monorail, we are situated so nicely in the warm car. We are escaping reality again. We are not telling each other the things that need to be said, like, "Sky still has a problem. I'm not okay. Nothing is okay." I stay quiet and look out at the Disney trees, so tall, so green.

We're only three hours from home, but this place feels so timeless to us. It has a centripetal force that pulls us in. We always come back. It's always the same. My brother starts to fall asleep. We're heading toward the center. We seek something on this monorail, the one-way track to where we always knew we'd go. I never see him anymore, I never get to spend any time with him. I'm so caught up in just being with him, the wonderful unrelenting love I have for my brother, that I forget about the wreckage ahead, what will happen when we leave Orlando.

Mom and I can't look at each other. The faces of other families blur into the afternoon. His dose of Seroquel kicks in and he will struggle the rest of the day. We're at full speed though, riding it out. I can feel his eyes snapped shut like a Lego brick when it gets stuck to another, an unmovable clump that gets lost in the bottom of the bin. Not even the fireworks exploding can wake us up from our stupor.

A Brief History of Partying

"You should bring a pair of socks for later," Dad says before I leave to attend my first bar mitzvah party. I'm twelve and some of the kids in my grade are already thirteen, most of them Jewish, and so there will be a lot of bar and bat mitzvahs this year. This is the first, though, and I am in a black dress and heels and I'm in a phase where I try to straighten my hair but the back always ends up bumpy. In pictures, it looks like I'm wearing a hat of my own hair that's too big for my head.

"No one does that!" I yell back, even though I've never been and don't know that for sure. The only bar mitzvah I've ever been to was my brother's, and his was special because we went to Israel for it. He never had a big party like this. We celebrated it as a family on top of Masada, far away from everyone we knew.

"Everyone does! And you'll be glad you brought them. What do you think happens after the service when it's time to dance? You think everyone dances in their shoes? Everyone takes them off for Coke and Pepsi and the Electric Slide. Do they still do that?"

"I don't know! Probably not." But they do. At every single one I attend all these games are played, and all in socks and not dress shoes or high heels.

It's Adam something-or-other's bar mitzvah and my best friend and I have arranged so that we don't go to the service, like jerks, and only go to the reception. "You only go to the service if it's your good friend or family member," I say with authority as the only Jew in the car. My friend's mom scribbles into her checkbook and hands it over. Twenty-five dollars. "It's supposed to be in increments of eighteen. *Chai* or double *chai*," I say. She waves us out of the car, tells us to have fun and call her cell phone when we're ready to leave. She pulls away and we stand on the sidewalk for a minute, eyeing our similar black dresses and heels, but her hair is crimped, which is also a thing now, and she's got my baby blue eyeliner on. I put black eyeliner on the inside of my bottom eyelids.

Inside there is a cocktail hour going on and adults are getting drunk and kids are saying "hi" to each other and pulling at their tights and shirt collars. The theme is Under the Sea, so half-naked mermaid women and funny-looking pirate men meander about and collect our envelopes and tell us to have a good time. When it's time for the big reception, Adam comes out in a suit with dancers to a choreographed routine and we take our seats at the assigned tables. Two boys pull us under the table and pass around a highball glass filled with clear bluish liquid. We take turns sipping and I realize this is alcohol. One of the boys says he collected half-finished drinks from glasses during the cocktail hour and dumped them all into one. Magic Potion.

I imagined a party being something different. I forgot about the chance that someone might become drunk, that kids would care about getting messed up and hooking up rather than getting dessert from the fondue fountain or customized temporary tattoos. If you danced with a boy, there was the promise of something sexual. If you got too drunk and threw up in the hotel pool, you caused a scene and your parents had to come get you. I didn't want any of this to happen.

Later, everyone takes off their shoes and plays Coke and Pepsi. I think of the stack of invitations on my desk that I had RSVP'd "Yes" to already. I think of all the dresses and all the socks in my future.

The black game console is always waiting for your return. It sits on the floor obedient and ready to entertain. Red wire to red socket. Yellow to yellow. White to white. Unravel the cords from around each controller. Plug them in. Push start.

Little colored karts buzzing, engines roaring, red hat, green hat, gold crown, dinosaur head, and mushroom face in the back. Lakitu holds the traffic light on a fishing pole from his station, his fluffy, digitized Mario cloud.

On the third siren, push the "A" button, hold it down, blast off into the rivalry, race past all the others. Nip Luigi in his side, swipe an item block, resist the urge to slide your pointer finger around the controller and press "Z," let it be a surprise, let the lottery of item choices spin, magic mushroom, green shell, red shell, then you get a star, cruise by the rest of the pack attacking each player in your way, they fly out left and right when you tap them, just a mere graze and they're gone, poof, out onto the edges of the screen.

I am coming home high for the first time. I am driving and have to pull over at a gas station and ask for directions to Woodfield Country Club where I live. I know the way, but my brain can't process roads. This is before the iPhone and GPS. I call Mom and she recommends asking for directions. I tell her I am lost. I say people were smoking at a party and I inhaled the air in the room, so I must have gotten affected. She says this makes no sense. She just wants me to come home.

The man at the gas station tells me to head east. I ask him to point and he does. I go that way for a while until I recognize the roads. I drive my brother's old BMW with the radio off the whole way home. When I get to the gate, I feel like I've accomplished something in my life, something big, something great.

Mom takes me into my bathroom and looks at my eyes. She knows. She sends me into Skyler's room. She tells me she will talk to me in the morning, when it wears off, and she leaves. We play video games. Skyler starts up Mario Party and I am losing horribly. I have no idea what is going on and I'm laughing at the spinning blocks instead of head-butting them and finding out how many spaces I need to move.

"How the fuck did you drive?" He asks.

"I had to pull over and ask a gas station attendant where Woodfield was."

"What happened?"

"He didn't know. But he said to go east. I knew I had to go east."

This elicits a large cackle from Skyler, one of the deep ones that is produced in his belly and comes out hazard-ously up through his throat. I'm pleased with myself. I've never smoked weed before. There was a bong at a house in Coral Springs and I hit it, many times, not knowing that once is enough. I stood outside for a few minutes and coughed. I almost threw up and then my breathing went back to normal. Someone on the couch was talking about how you are never by yourself because you're "with your-self" when you're alone. It made perfect sense to me until I got in the car and had to navigate the South Floridas alone. Not even Mom could help through the phone. Not even the gas station attendant. I was alone.

"I don't think you'll get punished," he says, picking up a star from the Wizard.

"How did you already get a star?"

"Because I'm playing and you're not!"

"You don't think she'll kill me tomorrow?"

"No, because I'm here. But don't drive if you're high. I could have gotten you."

"I was all the way in Coral Springs!" I inch back against his blue bed, the same one from childhood, the same one I've watched many a Mario match from. He's above me in his swivel chair. He's not even supposed to be home. He's right though. Mom can't kill me if he's here. He's my protector. He's my guardian.

"That would have taken me fifteen minutes, tops." He nods at the controller and I pick it up to play again. I'm starting to come down. I'm starting to see straight again.

We play until I feel fine enough to go to sleep. I ask if everything will go back to normal tomorrow because it seems foggy now, like I'm on Benadryl, like a sickness. He says it will be fine, that I'll be okay. He says he's going to stay up and that he's here if I need him. I shut the door behind me. His TV emits light from under the door. It shines a path from his room to mine, showing me the way.

Finish your laps quickly, faster than everyone else even though you're smaller, little Toad in his denim vest and happy smile, push Yoshi into the wall, shoot Bowser down with a red shell, always gaining speed, always pursuing the Mushroom Cup, always in the lead. Pick up a magic mushroom and tap tap tap tap tap tap tap tap tap tap tap tap tap until it runs out, until you can glide the joystick with ease, until you are flying. Press "R" and do a hop over the finish line, your time illuminated in big, bubble letters on the screen, Toad waving from his kart, the others coming in slow, one by one, and you gloat, you throw down your controller and watch the colors swirl.

I'm invited to a lingerie party at Jean Pierre's house in Boca Raton because I sell weed to the popular kids. J.P. and his high-class friends want my weed because it's from California and my brother gets it sent to him biweekly. My brother's in the depths of his addiction, and so am I. I am partying every weekend at someone else's house and my first real boyfriend just broke up with me because he wanted to date someone else for a while, then break up with her.

I'm supposed to meet a guy here who plays on the football team and is a big pothead. He heard about my special blend. I come to the party with a girl I don't know very well and don't like very much, but she wants to be popular and she wants to go to the party. She refuses to wear lingerie though, and I tell her she will look ridiculous. I don't like her because she's too quiet, and when I'm stoned, quiet people make me uneasy, like I'm falling down a dark hole void of sound.

We park and I stash the little baggies in my purse waiting to hand them out like Valentines. Get the cash, give it back to Skyler, keep a cut of it, everyone's happy. I've recently stumbled upon a bunch of Dad's old CDs and it's all I've been listening to. The Grateful Dead, Led Zeppelin, Spirit, which is my favorite right now. I play "Fresh Garbage" everywhere I go. I borrowed a white lace-up bustier from a girlfriend who can't attend the party and wear a white hoodie over it. I have to look the part if I'm going to show up and sell these kids some drugs.

Skyler's in Miami. He was doing just fine in grad school until his roommates became cocaine dealers. When they're not home and there's a knock on the door, Skyler answers and completes the transaction. That's how he falls into it. But something must have always been there inside, waiting to be awakened. "Hey, you wanna do a line?" Sniff sniff.

The party is magnificent. There are scantily clad high school girls parading around in cliques and the boys are in their silk underwear and robes smoking cigars. A stripper comes in at some point and pours alcohol all down her body for J.P. to proudly lap up. My friend likes J.P.'s best friend. He's wearing a tie with no shirt on. He's the one that pays me. My friend goes silent at the sight of him. I do most of the talking. Girls are already strewn about the couches looking vodka-logged with nipples showing. I find the guy I'm supposed to talk to and he's too stoned for his own good. He seems to like me and wants to go somewhere quiet to talk.

The guy my friend likes and my guy are friends somehow. They have a mutual respect for each other because one is a lineman for our football team and the other is rich, both showing signs of prosperity in their futures. The rich one says he knows a place. We walk toward my car, the four of us, my lineman in sweatpants holding my hand already. On the way, the most popular girl in the senior class appears. She's hanging out of a Ford F-150 with her boyfriend, another football player, and they're making out vigorously. She's in a beautiful silk kimono and a bra with high heels. She sees us cross her path and stops us like the Queen of Hearts. Her boyfriend grabs her by the ass and pulls her back in. She pushes him away in disgust and then gives him a look of endearment.

"Hey!" she calls out. "Didn't what's-his-face just break up with you?" She is asking me but everyone else is listening.

"Yes," I answer, shocked. I've only made eye contact with her once when I was running late to class because juniors and seniors traverse the same halls. She was wearing red high top Converse that I now own as well.

"He's an idiot. You're great! You're like smart and shit and he," she said, pointing to my new guy, "is way better. He's so cute! Good for you!"

Her boyfriend mumbles something incoherent.

"Shut the fuck up, no one cares what you think!" She snaps. Then she leans in and looks at me with her drunken eyes. "You're gonna be great." The prettiest girl in school, the richest girl, the cream of the crop.

We tear away from the party as the rich guy leads us to his parents' house that's still under construction. I let him drive my car because I'm too high at this point, especially as we pass around a joint, my girlfriend refusing to smoke it, but I don't mind her anymore. I'm back here with a guy's hand on my leg and it's all right. The mood is changing, and the farther we get away from the party the better I feel. I'm happy we're going to see where the house is being built. I'm happy we'll be somewhere where no one is.

The place is a disaster, like Roman ruins. The rich kid disappears for a few minutes and returns in a golf cart. He takes us to the top of the plot of land. We can see all of Boca from here. All the shimmering lights, the glistening man-made lakes, the sparkling chandeliers from inside glass windows reflecting toward us on the top of the hill. I know I don't belong here, that it happened by chance because I'm a girl of a certain age with certain curiosities. But it feels good to be so out of place. If I keep this up, I can really go places.

Toad stands on the podium, the scores tally and come together and he gets first place. You watch him hold up the trophy, the oversized gold prize, and he smiles back at you and says "I'm the best!" and you know it's true, you know that you're an unbeatable team, you and him, you can take on anyone. You win, you always win, but you need to keep playing because you always win.

Part of my sorority's hazing process is known as Sober Sister where we have to pick up drunk girls from the bars between the hours of 12:00 and 3:00 a.m. We have a big pledge class, so each of us only has to do it once, but we do it in pairs. I get stuck with my roommate who is afraid of cars and driving, being from New York, so that means

I have to do all of it. Maybe answering the phone is worse though, the sloppy yells and belligerent insults. My biggest fear is that one of the girls will get sick in my car. Each trip involves me racing back toward North Jordan as fast as I can. I know the shortcuts. I know I can cut across Fee Lane and turn right, then left, pull in by the side door and let them out. So far no one's gotten sick, but one girl did eat popcorn in my back seat and spilled it everywhere, I presume on purpose.

When we're not getting calls, we sit downstairs in the informal room and watch TV on the big screen. My room-mate does her homework and I try to write, since I've re-cently discovered I have a passion for it and now it's all I can do. I write about her while she sits beside me on the couch in one of my small notebooks and it gives me great joy to take notes on the way her face scrunches up involuntarily. I also write about the girls who stayed in or came back early and are eating loudly in the kitchenette whispering drunk-en banter between them. I like how ridiculous they are. Their outfits. Their hair. The boys they are inviting over to sleep with. I like how they think tonight matters so much.

Being in a sorority is nice because there are always people around to do things with. It's like having a hundred sis-ters who are all really pretty and dress well. I'm in a Jewish sorority, but aside from Passover dinner and the cultural history, it mostly just means we are a bunch of slutty girls who like to smoke weed. All the fraternities love us because we're little and cute, and we like to get high, but they also hate us because we leave parties early and complain a lot. This is why most of our older members go to the bars once they turn twenty-one.

I stopped talking to my brother when he got kicked out of where he was staying, something about getting caught for possession. He says it was prescribed, but I wasn't there and I don't know the whole story, and when it happened, I was about to start my sophomore year of college in Indiana. I wanted to focus on myself and stop worrying about him and everyone back at home. I knew that if he didn't want to help himself, that if he kept going because our parents wanted it and didn't do it for his own good, it wouldn't work. I'm going home in a few weeks for winter break and I'm not sure if I'll even see him.

The girls eventually head upstairs to meet their suitors or to send themselves to sleep. In the dark of the informal room, I can only hear my roommate's pencil marking up her paper. She's taking notes for something, but what she's doing looks pointless, like she's doing it to keep herself busy. It's almost 3:00 a.m. We'll be done soon. I can go to bed and then wake up and keep moving forward. The phone rings and we have to drive to a house party in the Villas, just outside Bloomington. Two girls scream into the phone and I grab my keys. "Come get us!" they say. "Hurry!"

In the Forest

Spin in circles in my denim jacket, watch the maple seeds fall from the trees, twirl down from the sky. Little helicopters. Pick them off the ground. Pinch them in the middle and stick them on my nose. Search for honeysuckle. Pop them open and kiss the insides. Drink the honey and collapse in the leaves. October in New York.

The kids in my kindergarten class hog the tire swing. I lace my fingers through the chain-link fence and watch the older kids play tennis. In the back of our playground, behind the big maple trees, there is a path that our teacher takes us on sometimes, a nature walk. We have to walk in pairs and hold hands with our neighbor. Harry Goldberg tells me that when we go in the forest, once we pass over the big tree stump, we are in heaven. It always seems to get quiet on that part of the walk, and I wonder if we are really dead. I think death is giant trees and rustling leaves. I imagine God sitting somewhere in the forest, waiting for us.

My brother was nine when he got pneumonia. He was a little kid, tiny frame, lean arms, fluffy puff of hair. I was four—just a small thing—people used to call me Itty Bitty Britty. I disliked it, but it was attention, so I took it. All press is good press. Everyone knew me as Skyler's little sister. Teachers welcomed me into their classrooms, remembering their days with my brother, the "A" student, the big deal, the next whiz kid, the future genius, their star student. I had my beautiful braid and array of colorful sweaters to set me apart from the crowd. There was one with fake fruit hanging off of it, pom-poms that I would suck on when no one was looking. The only time Skyler and I crossed paths at school was for picture day when siblings were encouraged to take their school photos together to be hung up on refrigerators or placed in the yearly look-how-they've-grown frames. He sat behind me, our hands folded on the makeshift table. The photographer shouted, "SAY CHEESE!" and the big white light flashed into our eyes. Then we separated, Skyler going one way and me back to the other side of campus.

He woke up coughing. *A cough isn't so bad*, I thought, *what's the big deal?* I can make myself cough if I try real hard. I can run the hot water and stick the thermometer under it. I can pretend I have a fever too. He had never lied, though; all nine years, a crystal-clear slate of innocence and perfect report cards.

My family went to see Dr. Judy in the city. We drove an hour to her office. I sat in the backseat with Mom while Dad drove and Skyler slept in the front, coughing in spurts the whole way. I looked out the window and watched the raindrops. I imagined them as a family, split apart by the rain and trying to swim back together. They bounced and rolled down the window, tumbling and connecting, then became dismembered and torn apart again. I put my finger up to the ones I wanted to be joined. I waited to see if my finger alone could draw them together. Mom told me to take my hands off the glass.

We waited two hours to be told that Dr. Judy was unsure of the diagnosis. I remember her floppy white lab coat, her frizzy blond hair gathered up in a big scrunchie on top of her head, the waiting room with the wooden play center, moving the red balls and orange cubes and the yellow triangles along their paths. I remember Andes chocolates from the glass jar in the waiting room. I never liked them, but my brother did.

He kept getting worse. He wasn't one to miss school, so even his teachers were concerned. I wasn't allowed in his room. I wanted in. He had all the good books in there, all the ones I couldn't even read yet. I narrated my own stories from the pictures. And he had all the Legos, the board games, the video games. I had the Barbies. Those dumb rubbery girls who never talked back. I once burned one of their heads on the stove. Mom helped because I was too young to use the kitchen appliances. I said it was a way to express myself, so she let it happen. I had one doll that I called the "ugly doll." She was used for experiments, tortured, cut, burned, painted, dyed. The rest would stay well-dressed and beautiful.

My friends all had the accompanying Ken dolls so that Barbie could go on dates. On play dates, I would dress up the dolls. They would have a lovely evening together and kiss at the end. At home, I could put my dolls in danger and see what happened to them when they were pushed to the edge of death.

A memory. We are at a school play. *The Lion, the Witch, and the Wardrobe.* Mom wanted us to go. The three of us are sitting there. My brother and I lean back in our chairs. We feel our heads get hot. We are kids. We are sick kids. We feel ourselves burning up like heat waves in the New York summer. Our little heads, our little bodies, growing sick, each scene melts into another, each scene brings us closer to our end. Mom notices there is something wrong, so we leave early. At the intermission, we make a break for it. Skyler takes the front seat, reclines all the way. I spread my mini self in the back, looking up at the roof of the car. Everything is boiling. My mouth feels hot. We complain of the same condition. It's Thursday. There won't be school for us tomorrow, us sick kids. We need medicine to make us better. We need good night sleeps and lots of apple juice. We separate at home; Skyler in his blue room, me in my pink room. I watch a marathon of some cartoon show about rotten tomatoes. They're evil and they steal things from science labs, and I drink juice boxes, one after another, throwing them on my carpeted floor when I'm done. I'm resting in my room. I'm sleeping through the day and up all night watching these glowing, red tomatoes fight the city. My brother is on the other side of the house. He battles the sickness in another way. This way I do not know and will never see because we are separated. We are sliding down the window, small raindrops torn apart. In the middle of the night, I wake up choking for air, my head still hot, beads of sweat rolling down, raindrops on fire. From the other side of the house, I hear noises. Sometimes I hear him coughing. Sometimes I hear nothing.

My parents took him to the hospital. I still had to go to school, and I only got to have one of my parents home at night. Sometimes I stayed with Grandma and she made me eat orange muffins. I only liked blueberry.

Mom waited by his bedside while Dad had to work. Visitors came and went. I was oblivious, only worried about which sticker I'd get for putting my backpack and crayons away correctly or how many minutes I'd get to play on the tire swing. I had to wear my hair down every day because Mom was so occupied with Skyler. Everyone wondered where my beautiful braids went. I liked the way my hair flew free, running down the big concrete hill at school.

In the hospital room in the middle of the night, Mom got up to go to the bathroom. When she came back, some nurses were wheeling my brother away. The nurses made a mistake in taking the wrong boy, and luckily Mom had been there to intervene.

This chaos caused Dad to come in the next day and make a scene. The mishap was cleared up, but my parents wanted him out of the New York University Hospital.

Sensei Paul visited. He was my brother's karate instructor. He rubbed Skyler's back, moved around the mucus and phlegm, loosened his muscles. He wanted Skyler back in the dojo as soon as he felt well again. He was training to earn a black belt.

Then I visited. This hospital was big. Not that I had been to any other, but the lobby was huge and everything felt oversized. Murals painted by children lined the walls. Big glass windows let in the daylight. Lab coats rustled, and ink pens jotted down notes. I held Dad's hand.

"Skyler doesn't look so good," he warned me.

"What do you mean?"

"He looks sick."

I had only seen television episodes of sick kids in bed. I imagined my brother with two black eyes and a bloody face. A kid in a wheelchair started coughing a few feet away from us. I looked up and saw a giant papier-mâché ball that had the whole world painted on it. I felt like Indiana Jones in *Raiders of the Lost Ark*. It was going to break off and fall any moment. I closed my eyes and saw my brother dying. I felt the hospital grow around me, I felt the forest, the trees, the tall maples mocking, everything larger than I was, bigger than I could ever be, greater than I could possibly understand.

I let go of my Dad's hand and started crying, silently at first. When he tried to pull me along, I threw a fit. It was too much for me to handle. I could only take my burning Barbies, exploding tomatoes, and the bubbling orange river of Bowser's castle. That's what pain was to me. That's what I knew about death.

Skyler eventually got better and came home. He went back to fight in karate, I got Mom to braid my hair again for school, and civilization was restored. But that day at the hospital I realized something awful could happen to someone I loved. Before, I only knew of creepy crawlers and beautiful dolls, the anxiety of my family watching *Jeopardy* or *Wheel of Fortune* together in the living room, Mario falling off Rainbow Road, and little Lakitu in his cloud, bringing Mario back to life.

Another memory. Mom used to sew us plush Mario stars made out of felt. She drew faces on them with Sharpies. When we moved, she made me one of an apple to represent New York, and one of an orange to represent my new life in Florida. I stitched the orange myself. My brother didn't want an orange. He just kept his yellow star. It was Skyler's idea for us to make the characters from the game; he wanted them to be real. He loved the cute little stars, and because he had one, I had to have one, too.

The plastic bin of our plush toys sits in the center console of the car on the way to see Grandpa for the last time before we move. Mom had been working on them while we were at school. The edges of my orange are uneven, and it makes me sad. I want a good orange. I want my orange to look as good as the apple. Mom doesn't seem right. She keeps missing the turn and can't figure out where to park. She doesn't let us say goodbye to our grandpa. Instead, she just leaves the car running in front of his apartment building, the building she grew up in, the building where she had babysat for a serial killer, the building where bad things happen to good people. My brother and I sit in the car, Skyler on his Game Boy and me staring at the fruits and stars and holding them, poking their bellies, pulling at the stitches, hoping I could get my little orange fixed. Mom comes back crying. She has to leave her dad. Skyler and I stay quiet. We aren't sure how to deal with leaving people, what the protocol is for this kind of thing. She puts the soundtrack to *Footloose* on, slips the cassette tape in, turns it up loud, as loud as it goes, and the music is blasting, and she is crying, and my brother starts screaming. "You're crazy! You're crazy! Turn it off!" I want to look back at him, to see what he thinks, to see what he feels, if he is as scared as I am. But I can't move. I want to turn around and grab the sleeve of his coat, make him understand that I don't want any part of this, that maybe he and I could run away, get out of town, be the pair we are meant to be, genius and willing accomplice, brother and sister.

My brother is twenty-eight, and I am twenty-three. I am living at home because Los Angeles didn't work out. He writes a suicide letter, an incoherent mix of song lyrics and memories from the past. He posts it online with a picture of himself, a gun and a cigarette. After that, he goes missing. Friends that he hasn't spoken to in years call our house looking for him. I trip over my Nintendo 64 console to answer the call at 3:00 a.m. from a college friend. He tells me to go on Facebook. I tell him I don't have one. He lets me use his information to log on and see for myself.

We can't get ahold of Skyler for a while. I think he is dead; I'm sure of it. I know that when he sets his mind to something, he always goes through with it. I try to recall the last time we saw each other. I think about going to Dave & Buster's for dinner and arcade games a few months ago. I remember thinking he was high again but not really caring because I just was so happy to spend time with him. He calls Mom back around 4:00 a.m. Mom and I drive down to pick him up with no plan. Maybe something will come to us on the way, but it doesn't. We just silently hope he doesn't do anything before we get there.

He packed a bag: six 24-ounce red Gatorade sports bottles, a stack of black and white speckled notebooks (filled cover to cover with his writing), a change of clothes, all of his medication, and a small, silver handgun.

He walks out of the sliding glass doors. We hug him and drive home. Once we get back, Skyler sleeps on the couch for a few hours, still under the influence. I go back to sleep as well, shut off my phone and wake up before he does. I watch him sleep. My mom has put his childhood, blue blanket over him. He still might be dead. The pills might be traversing through his system in a bad combination of ways. He might not wake up. He might not be sleeping, but drifting off into that other place. He lies there in perpetual motion. We're all dying now because he wants to die. Leaves rustle as he turns over.

I decide to go for a run and clear my head. When I open the front door, a police officer stands there about to knock on our door. He asks if Skyler is home. After the officer asks him a few questions and takes his gun, Skyler walks out to the terrace to think things over. He smokes cigarette after cigarette, filling up the ashtray, overflowing, pacing back and forth in his black jacket. Sweat is pouring off his forehead. He calls someone to come get him. When I come home from my run, he is still out there, waiting, waiting for something to pull him out of this life and into the next. Mom drags me outside and tells me to say goodbye. I know she can't handle this anymore, the worrying, the suspense—and she just wants it to be over. I know what she means. I can't handle it either. I can't keep holding my breath for my brother. She leaves us out there for a while. I realize that this may be the last time I will ever see him in the flesh. The prodigy. The only brother I have. I start crying.

"I really want a brother," I say.

"I'm sorry, Britt. I just don't want to live."

I hug him. I don't want to live anymore either. But I have to go to work. I have to move on with my life, like I have before, without my partner, without my brother. I begin to realize that death is real, and it is sitting on our terrace chain-smoking.

He leaves the house before I get home. A few days later he goes missing again. This time, the cops get to him first, before the pain pills have time to kick in. They Baker Act him and put him in the hospital for a week.

It's the end of October. My brother is out of the hospital now, and everything that happened is almost last month's news. But I am the one that will carry it forever. I will be the one that opened my front door to an officer, saw the silver gun glisten in his backpack, said goodbye to my brother before he again attempted to end his life.

Everyone's selling pumpkin-flavored everything. I stop at a breakfast place to have a pumpkin bagel and pumpkin cream cheese. I want to sit and enjoy this meal, not having eaten much all week, and I'm finally alone now. No police. No phone calls. No family chaos. I spread a lot of cream cheese on the bagel, it's so sweet, even too sweet, and it reminds me of the apple juice, just like our childhood, and there was always too much of everything. Our backpacks were always full. Our clothes were layered on for the New

York cold. Our heads were kissed and bodies tucked into fluffy comfortable beds. Our lives were so abundant.

There were days when I wanted to be better. Back in college, I got a job waitressing at a sushi restaurant so I could pay for weed and clothes and the house I rented with my three best friends at the time. I would tie on my apron, change out of my boots, put my sneakers on, and really want that big table, work for that big tip, make the big money and be okay on my own out there. I was in Indiana, finishing up my senior year, and all of it felt so wrong. Every time my shoes slid into the snow or I took a sip of whiskey at the bar on a Tuesday night, I felt like I was moving further and further away from everything I wanted. I was always staring at people, trying to see who they were, never doing the same with myself, but I could imagine whole lives of people, whole stories, entire lifetimes. Some days, I would stare out the window at work and think about jumping. My body would land hard on the snowy pavement. My manager would find my body. But there were days when I felt optimistic. I could reason that if I graduated, finished, got out of there, I could start over.

One day when I'd had enough, I went into my bathroom and emptied the cabinets. I had medication left over from a surgery I had that past summer: Valium, Oxycodone, Xanax . . . I hooked my fingers around the pills, put them in my mouth, one by one, and felt like I was finally going somewhere, moving to that place where I could be better.

My friends were outside on the porch, drinking before the Little 500, the big bicycle race on campus, and when I realized I didn't want to die, I called to one of them. I said, "Call Skyler, call my brother, call him." I hadn't talked to him in four years, aside from "Hello" or "Happy Birthday." I could never handle his addiction, so I distanced myself so far that I was now grazing the edge of death. She called him and handed me the phone. I fell down on my bed, the effect of the pills already set in motion. I looked out the window, melted snow on the ground, the day slowly turning into evening, the sky collapsing into night, and I pressed the phone to my ear. His voice shot through the other side.

"Hey, Britt, are you there?"

Smoke cigarettes on the porch until I feel okay. Indiana trees shift back into focus, their loud whistling, their swaying branches. Leaves fall into the wet street. Watch them soak up rainwater. The effect of the pills dissipates. The biggest tree at the end of the block towers over the houses on the street. Maybe it's God. Maybe He has come.

Birthday Girl

I am turning twenty-three today at 10:30 a.m. I have to work, so I stop at McDonalds even though I know it will make me late. I don't care because I hate my job. I don't really hate my job, I just hate working there and being there and not getting to be creative with my writing. I'm at a point where the money is so good and the living is so nice that it's extremely hard for me to find a way out.

I order an egg and cheese sandwich on a biscuit and orange juice. I am fifteen minutes late to work and I throw away the greasy bag before entering the office building. It's a high-rise on Wilshire, right next to the LACMA and walking distance to the La Brea Tar Pits. I've become accustomed to walking there every day on my hour lunch break, sitting on a bench, sometimes even lying down and looking up at the blue, blue sky. It's always 70 degrees and sunny. There are children on field trips learning about dinosaurs and exploring the Tar Pits. There are families having picnics on the table. This is where I think about killing myself, when morning turns to afternoon and I know it will soon be night and I will be alone again. I have a fur coat and expensive shoes in my closet. I can buy whatever

I want and go anywhere, as I often tell myself, but I stay here for some reason, on the bench, attempting to call my mom and tell her all of this, but getting too choked up and saying "I have to go, lunch is over." Then I take my time walking back, looking for a good food truck on the street, getting hot chocolate instead and sitting in the lobby on the carpeted floor before I have to go back.

None of this on my birthday though. Today I wear a floral dress and a fawn colored cardigan with my hair down, new boots, the greenish grayish leather ones I ordered online. Today there is happiness because the office wants to get me a cake and asks me what kind I like. They're going to have a production assistant go out and buy one before the day is over. There will be candles and singing and ice cream cake from Carvel, which is my absolute favorite. Today I am the birthday girl and it is all for me.

My mom texts me at 10:30 a.m. on the dot and I cry at my desk because I'm nowhere near her. My officemates know that I'm going through something, but they don't know what and they're too busy to really ask about it and get involved. I don't want them to anyway, and especially not today, my birthday and all. "They're getting you a cake, you know" one says. "That's a big deal," says the other.

At lunch I go to the burger place where you can "create your own" burger. I order a turkey burger on a wheat bun with sweet potato fries and a vanilla shake. It's all so rich and tasty and a few friends call while I'm eating to wish me a happy birthday. "What are you doing today?"

they ask and I see my reflection in the bar mirror. "Eating French fries alone," I reply, and they laugh because I'm the funny, sarcastic friend that lives in LA now, and they're in Chicago or still in Indiana or maybe back home in Florida at their 9-5 that they love and it's totally working and they feel a part of things there, they really fit in.

The key to get into the office is on a separate key holder that I bought on Melrose, a giant mouth that looks like a chattering teeth wind-up toy with red fleshy lips and white, white teeth that unzip to reveal a pink tongue inside. Back in the office I watch episodes of a TV show for a promo we are doing but I don't take notes, I just watch. My big headphones are on and I can't hear anyone in the office as they plan where to put my cake and what time to sing to me. There is a feeling that today is all about me, an illusion that I create, a simulation of what a "birthday" is and that I'm supposed to feel "special." But I still feel like dying. I feel like I came here to LA and now I know too much. I know what happens inside of offices and how things get from videotape onto a television screen, a movie screen, how an idea takes shape and transforms to become a box-office hit. I know how long it takes to realize someone won't call you back, and then how long it takes them to text you in the middle of the night because they thought about you because you really are "special." I know what the inside of a hot nightclub looks like on a Saturday, on a Tuesday, at the VIP table, on the dance floor. I know the drive from here to Newport, from here to San Diego, from here to the Hollywood Hills and out past the Valley and Ventura, from here to anywhere out there that I can go because I have money and all the time in the world. It's sad though. It is a sad, sad thing to be able to see the world when you are so miserable. My officemate stands in front of my desk and signals me that it's time for cake.

The icing is blue on the white cake. "Happy Birthday" with some colored jelly balloons. No name underneath. The PA didn't know my name because she's new. People sing to me. I stand there in my dress waiting to blow out the candles on a cake that is for me, but without a name it could be for anyone, and so I decide it's for all of us. We all need the cake and the happy birthday song and so I even sing along a little. I lean over and blow out the candles. I am served the first piece, a big square with icing and sprinkles and a pink balloon.

My boyfriend wants to spend my birthday with me. We technically broke up many times since I've been in LA, but I remember the day he came back from Vegas and put a note in one of my Reese's Cups in the fridge asking if I would be his girlfriend. I almost didn't find it because I insisted that I wasn't hungry and didn't want to eat the candy yet, but he said, "Fine, I'll have one, open it for me" so I opened the package and the note was inside somehow already. He's not really my boyfriend, but he is in some ways. We spend a lot of nights together. We watch a lot of movies. We are sad together and don't admit it because the presence of another person can sometimes make you feel happier for a time.

He comes over after work in his black Chevrolet and hands me a card, oddly enough the same exact one my mom had sent me in the mail this week. It is Mickey Mouse on the front wishing me a happy birthday and holding a bouquet of balloons. We drive into Westwood and get pizza, my favorite, have beer at the bar next door and then go home back to my place.

My apartment is a studio that looks promising or plaintive, depending on the light. It's one room with a separate little area for the bathroom and a kitchen around the corner. There's a balcony, which is everything, but it overlooks the parking garage. Still, it's hosted many wine nights and strange men. Many joints have been smoked on my couch and many cigarettes have been shared on the balcony. I tried to hang lights during the holiday time, but gave up because I was too stoned and tired.

From the shower he yells and reminds me of the ecstasy we have left over from New Year's. We never ended up doing it; we got too drunk and stumbled to Santa Monica beach to watch fireworks. It was so cold that we couldn't hold our bottle of whiskey and had to bury it in the sand. I take the white capsules out of my drawer in the bathroom. They're in a Ziploc bag next to my hair ties. I scored them from a kid who lives in my building, which is mostly UCLA students with a lot of money who like to do drugs. He is also in love with me but I don't like him because his upper lip is always sweaty and he consistently smells of hot dogs. I kissed him once and we watched a movie about modern-day vampires, but now he's just my drug dealer, or one of them.

I take a white pill out of the bag and he opens the shower curtain and flashes me. He sticks out his tongue and I pop the capsule and sprinkle the white powder on his tongue. "Now do yours quick!" He yells and finishes his shower.

When I moved to Los Angeles I was under the impression that everything would be just fine. Palm trees, pot, a real pleasure of a place for a twenty-two-year-old to frolic in and really get to know herself. The thing is I quickly developed a taste for all things previously forbidden and was making up for lost time. I've never done ecstasy before and don't know what to expect. He's already taken his dose though, so I take mine.

We decide to walk. We walk from my apartment down the hilly streets to Westwood Boulevard. We're in jackets in January. We move through town swiftly. I feel good all of a sudden, but I'm not sure if he feels it yet so I don't say anything. He says we should karate chop the air and so we do. He says he feels like something is happening, like it's working, and I agree, and then we're both excited. My ears pop and I can hear everything in the night. My shoes on the street, his hair moving in the wind, the neon lights of storefront signs. We beeline into CVS because he needs a lighter. I stand in line with him under the bright white lights. He wants to keep moving and I want to keep moving too. When we are standing still we feel too much, like our bodies are working out something inside and we can feel the gears clinking, the mechanism going.

We float around the city streets happy and alive. We find a gypsy woman who wants to tell my fortune. She says my friend must wait outside. I give her my palm.

"Someone in your life is not who they say they are."

"Is it him?"

"I'm not sure." But she looks at me like she is sure. I've never been more sure of someone else's certainty. I give her twenty dollars and feel different, like a weight has been placed, like a light has gone out, one that's so small it's almost unnoticeable.

We walk back to the apartment and take pictures and find souvenirs, which cheers me up as I can collect things in my pocket; a ribbon from a mailbox, crepe paper from a house party, a warning sign fallen on the ground. Back at my apartment we smoke a joint because it will make us feel better. We're both bored but can't admit it because the drug might take a bad turn if we do. We're lying to each other endlessly. We smoke pot inside and cigarettes outside because there needs to be a separation of the two. I can tell he wants to be alone on the balcony so I let him be, but I'm going crazy so I take out paper and markers and crayons and draw things until he gets back. He looks improved after he smokes, the color back in his face, he lies down on the carpet with me to draw and we laugh and it's better. He puts on music and we dance a little, then undress and make love and it's not my birthday anymore. It's well after midnight and I pour us two glasses of water that I force us to drink. I say I have vitamins for the morning that will help our bodies adjust. I'm not sure what it means, but my drug dealer told me to say it and I trust the science behind it.

In bed we exhibit a sort of restless tiredness that only comes from psychoactive drug use. We talk for a while and get the kinks out of our system, like smoothing out an unruly comforter. He falls asleep first. I stare at the walls, beige and boring, unaltered by me living there for eight months now. Stagnant, like me in Los Angeles.

I replay the day over and over in my mind. I almost feel like myself again. Then I realize I haven't spoken to my brother today. He didn't call me on my birthday. I wonder where he is and what he's doing. I wonder if he ever liked doing MDMA. I try to picture what tomorrow looks like, but it's filled with holes, and I can hear my brain shifting, refocusing, I can feel my mind still moving forward without me.

Much Needed Prayer

The sky opens up. I stare into the swirl of rain and lightning and try and catch my breath. He makes a phone call. The wind is howling. I ask the universe a question and I wait for the answer. When the meeting is over, I follow him.

The power goes out when the lightning hits. A tree branch barrels over. Blue and white sparks fly out of the transformer. I jump up in bed and run out into the living room. He was supposed to come to bed a while ago, but a movie was on and just shut off suddenly. He's not scared. He says it is God, showing us how powerful He is.

He lights a candle and it makes us look big on the walls. He says we should read a little more before going to sleep. He opens up with prayer and holds my hand while he works his way from his family's needs to mine, from his past to his present, from him to me, from me to God, from God forever on and on and on.

Summer. Delray Beach. We want to go out on the weekends to nightclubs and dance. He doesn't drink, but he likes to sip Red Bulls while I drink Red Bulls and vodka. He's still in a halfway house. The house mom doesn't like me because we close the door to his room when we watch movies. His roommates like me because I'm from the other world, the other side of the tracks, east of Military, east of I-95, all the way east of A1A. They like when I talk about God. They like that I'm hopeful and holding onto something, something I can't see or understand.

"It's good to not understand," I say. "If you understand that means you can grasp it. I want to believe in something I can't even fathom. Don't you?"

This is all discussed among cigarette after cigarette, but I don't smoke anymore. Occasionally I take a sip of Sprite and close the bottle back up meaningfully, as if I'd had enough. One guy here won't make it to next week. He's already relapsed and he's talking about going on a run, selling his amp and somehow getting his car back and taking it all the way to Jersey.

"As if anything good is happening in Jersey," the guy I'm seeing jokes. He actually knows my ex-boyfriend, another former junkie who turned a corner and now gets people into treatment, and as of now they hate each other, but in three months they will cross paths at the gym and realize they're meant to be friends. For now we shit talk the ex-boyfriend and I am in a good place because I'm winning. I'm helping people. I'm driving the van to meetings and picking up kids off the street. I'm telling people they should believe in something.

I'm all set to go to graduate school in the fall, get my Master of Fine Arts in creative nonfiction, and all these boys will become a part of my story. We go to the beach during the day and sit in a circle. No one goes in the water except me. I'm carefree and moving toward something better than where I've been. Even if I'm in the in-between, I know I'm heading out of it.

The last time we ever hang out we go to a club in Fort Lauderdale on a weekend. His mom pays for a hotel room and I pack a tight black dress. We meet some friends out and dance until 2:00 a.m. On the way back, my guy chain-smokes and tells me he almost has a year. Back at the hotel, he has a headache and lies supine on the bed, like a saint. I feed him Advil and Gatorade and declare it's dehydration, the heat, the Florida heat, the Florida summer has gotten to him.

"You're so nice," he says, eyes closed, about to drift off and dream of other things. I rub his temples and he falls asleep. I fall asleep in my dress next him.

"The deal's this," my new boyfriend says. It's how he always starts his sentences when we begin our relationship. Then he goes into the energies.

"Stay in the lightness. If you feel darkness ask the question, 'Who does this belong do?' Then shift it."

I nod, but inside I wonder, what if it belongs to me? What if it is mine? Then how do I adjust? I've spent the last few years running from my troubles, running from problems that might have been my own. Not the wrong city, not the wrong job. I was wrong. I was unable. I was unwilling. All this time I've been looking for someone to be my guide, like how my brother used to be, how he used to lead me and protect me and show me the way. Now I must do all that for myself. I've become my own sibling, my own parent, my own friend. I can't speak to him when he's living how he is, but I want my brother back, badly. I yearn for late night phone calls. Dinners. Holidays. Birthdays. Memories. I miss his laugh more than anything.

"Realizing I was wrong was the most freeing feeling," I say. He smokes and listens intently. I lean back in a chair on the porch and gaze into the night sky.

"The next part will be better," he answers, stamping out his cigarette in the ashtray and leaning in for a kiss.

When we break up, he tells me he will pray for me.

The Perpetual Motion Machine

An ex-boyfriend of mine flew in from Chicago. In California he had promised me Catalina. On the phone he said, "Key West." He flew down to Florida and we drove. We shared an egg and cheese croissant and coffee on the way down. He was out of a job and I was waitressing at a sports bar. I knew I'd be paying for the whole thing—the hotel room, the gas, the everything. I knew all the tips that had ever made their way into my green apron would disappear into the Florida Keys.

Near the end of the drive we come to a sparse stretch of bridges, each one looking less and less reliable. I eat an apple out of anxiety and think about the difference between skin and flesh, what we put out into the world versus what's really inside. As we ride over one of the bridges, I throw my apple as far as I can out the window and watch it land in the water. The car jerks because he wants to see where it lands. He wants to see the splash to know it has been a success. The car realigns and it's the kind of thing you hold your breath for. The kind of fear that makes you pray to God.

We check into the hotel and he needs a fax machine. He's moving again and needs to get some information to the landlord. He won't have cable TV in his next apartment. This is before he gets money again and makes a living taking pictures and selling ads and using drugs. Now he is in the lobby making out a letter to his soon-to-be roommate. He wears swim trunks and flip-flops back in the state he was raised in, but no one knows he is here except for me, not even his family who live a few hours north.

We came back to New York when I was finally old enough to get my birthmark removed. My parents wanted me to use the same laser surgeon who removed a wart from my finger in the second grade, the one with good bedside manner and a nice office in the city. Dad was still commuting, which made it convenient for us to stay with him in his hotel room, and Mom decided to make the trip a week long so I could recover before heading back to Florida.

The procedure was explained to me many times; the doctor would numb the area with a series of shots. This would hurt the most. "Every nerve below the skin has to be put to sleep," he said, trying to make me understand. All I knew was that I wanted the birthmark gone. I wanted to be able to wear bikinis at the pool and not get made fun of for having a giant circle on my side. I was eleven, and I didn't want to be the only girl in a one piece anymore. I wanted to be sexy.

The surgery hurt more than I anticipated. To this day, no pain resembles one quite like being awake while the doctor put each nerve to sleep, numbing them by setting them on fire, one by one. Some nerves never woke up and patches on my side remain numb and lifeless. The day before we headed back to Florida, Mom took Skyler and me to see the Statue of Liberty. We used to go a lot as kids, but I didn't remember how majestic she was, how green she was in person, like a hospital gown.

Mom went to buy tickets so we could ascend the statue. I kept feeling under my shirt at the bandages that were leaking. Mom kept looking back at us and seemed to be getting angry. I walked up to her and asked what was wrong.

"Go back over there!" Mom yelled.

I walked back over to Skyler.

"There's a sign that says no one can go up to the crown right now," Skyler said. "So Mom is probably arguing with the lady."

"Well, what are we going to do?" I asked.

"She'll figure something out," he said.

Just then, Mom came back over to us smiling.

"How did you do it this time?" Skyler asked.

"I told them Britt was terminally ill. So you better look real sick."

All those steps made my wound bleed even more, but it was worth it. There are pictures of me from that day in my baby blue eyeliner and a red headband, happy and smiling but hunched over a bit because of the pain.

On the first night in the Keys, after walking down Duval and taking in the pink sunset, we sit in the hotel room and watch reruns of old Disney Channel shows. He buys us some tall boys to drink by the pool and we decide to take ecstasy, like old times. I brought it because I knew he'd do it with me. I knew we would get to that point where we'd run out of sad stories and need to make some new ones.

It goes like this: He's happy when I wear the lime green sweatshirt. I keep it on even though I'm hot too. He can't seem to get his temperature right. He only wants the Gatorade poured into cups before drinking it. I'm by the mini fridge in the hotel room, rationing our supply, measuring the neon red liquid, trying to make it as even as possible. He takes a shower, insisting it will help. I just want him to jump in the pool and get his body cool again. He says this is the only way though, that the drugs have taken effect and he knows a hot shower will help. He steps out in a towel and says he feels better, but I know he doesn't quite yet. We lay on the bed and I put on music. He suggests some band I've never heard of, so I put it on and it's perfection. I'm in the exact center of the room and his head is in my lap, so he's in the middle too, and we're in the middle of something here, something greater than what either of us will ever know, an agreement with the universe that if we can get through tonight alive, we will repay it somehow, but without the pressure or confines of any kind of real contract, as this is sworn by simply closing our eyes and listening to the music vibrating in the room. I know it will all be okay in the end, but he doesn't. One person should always be the knower though, and one person should always be unsure, so that the other one can assure them. Underneath my sweatshirt, the strings of my bathing suit are too tight, but I know if I move, the whole thing will fall apart, this safe haven, this contract we've created between heaven and earth, this ever-circling sound of the acoustic guitar and some guy's voice who I don't know, rocking us gently like babies, telling us we've got a deal.

I got invited to an all-expense-paid trip to New York by an ex-boyfriend. We started dating in high school and were on and off for years, but we were so young, and it always seemed that we were meant to be friends rather than lovers. He broke up with me when he went to college, but we got back together when I attended the same university as him out in Indiana a year later. We took a break junior year and when I dated someone else for a while, he was never able to forgive me. He was a senior, all set to move to New York after graduation.

"I thought you'd meet me there in a year and we'd get married," he said before ending it between us. All I could think about was how I spent so much time dating guys and obsessing over "love." I didn't even know what I wanted out of life. I had no idea what I wanted the rest of my life to be.

But I was in a bad spot a few years ago, and he invited me to New York for the week. He paid for everything because I couldn't, and because he would never have made me pay anyway. He was always a gentleman, a nice Jewish boy, and despite everything that had happened between us years ago, he still cared about me, a lot. I didn't care about myself though, at all. I didn't know how to receive love, how to love myself.

When I arrived in New York, I dropped my bags off at his apartment. He tried to kiss me on his bed and I told him no. I said I wasn't capable of anything intimate, and I hoped he would understand. He nodded, and we left to grab dinner and see a show. He took me to see *Aladdin*, because Disney is and will always be my favorite, and I got peanut M&Ms and a Sprite. He got two glasses of wine that came in plastic collectable cups, but when I refused that too, he proceeded to drink both and then order another. The show was amazing, and the Broadway Theatre glowed gold and warm, a nice contrast to the cold outside, allowing me to be comfortable in my sweater. He kept drinking. I tried to stay focused on the genie's beautiful solo, the love story blossoming, thinking maybe I could "get in the mood," but I was still so sad from my recent break-up, I simply could not.

After the show we walked for a while and it became clear how drunk he was. He was slurring his words and tripping, so I said I'd pay for a cab.

"Ha! You're going to pay, that's rich!" He yelled at me on the sidewalk.

"I don't feel comfortable walking with you. Let's just hail a cab."

"Hail a cab? No one says that. You're just a dumb slut."

"That's not nice."

"Oh my God. You won't even DO anything. So it's not true. But you still are a slut. And a bitch."

"I'm getting a cab."

"Oh my God! I'll call an Uber. Like, don't worry."

We went back to the apartment where he smoked out of his bong, offered me some, and I got high. I hadn't smoked weed in four years. He passed out immediately and I got so high that I stayed up for hours watching *The Mindy Project* on his TV. I kept the volume on low so I wouldn't wake him up. It was so quiet in the city and in his apartment. Even though he apologized the next morning, the whole thing made me realize that maybe I wasn't the only one who was hurting. I had done things without self-awareness. I had acted out of desire. I wanted to be someone I wasn't good at pretending to be. I made a promise to myself to find out who I really was.

On the last day, we got coffee and walked around Central Park. I texted my ex back in Florida a picture of the cityscape and he said he missed me. I remember finding addresses of girls in his emails that he left open on his computer. It made me curious enough to read his bedside notebook and find out he wanted to sleep with a girl he worked with, a girl he would talk to at lunchtime, trying to get closer to her every day while eating the lunch I made for him. He asked when I would be back from my trip. He said he wanted to hang out and talk.

My ex and I decide to go on a guided snorkeling tour. The boat leaves at noon and we cross from South Street to Whitehead Street all the way down to the Marina. We pass Hemingway's house and take a photo in front. I now realize the tragedy that is Key West and how one can certainly go down the rabbit hole here, deeply. We approach a bar and decide to stop for a few drinks and a game of pool, which I win somehow, and then lose to him in a game of darts. The bar is quiet but some locals are getting their early morning drinks in.

It's not until the boat leaves the dock that I remember I get seasick. We stand away from everyone and watch the Keys fade away into a small strip thin as paper. We are away now. The catamaran is big enough that I don't feel sick at all and we get our gear on and line up to jump off the boat. I spit into my mask and rub in the saliva like my dad taught me to the first time I went snorkeling. It won't fog up this way. It will remain clear. We jump into the water. I follow him. We're supposed to stay within certain borderlines of the group but he traverses those boundaries and goes off on his own. He signals me over and below is a school of fish fluttering through a reef. Here we are, the two of us, doing things together like we always wanted, but something feels different about it, like it's too late. Like we had our chance. I swim away and go off on my own now. The water is warm and the sun shines on my back. I'm wearing a navy blue bikini that my mom picked out. She's not happy I went on this trip but at least she knows I'm here. And now I'm in the middle of the ocean, floating, feeling different, feeling alone.

Back on the boat we drink margaritas. I drink a lot because I want to feel better. He drinks a lot because he always does. There is a man next to us with his son who is about our age. They work in Boca Raton and come here a lot. The man is around fifty or so and has a firm belly, wears glasses, reminds me of my dad, but he's more outgoing and he puts his arm around his son when he talks. We cheers our drinks and talk and laugh. He's in publishing or sales or something like that and my ex is interested in a job down here in Florida instead of up north. Perhaps he's thinking about living his life the way we used to imagine. I'm designated as the re-filler of drinks and step away to retrieve more margaritas. I come back with cups by the twos and everyone seems happy and engaged in conversation. I'm happy we met this man and that he is talking to us and having a good time. This is how vacation is supposed to be. These nice people are the kind you are supposed to meet.

The boat pulls into the dock and we put our clothes on over our bathing suits. I'm drunk and I've just had a great afternoon. Maybe he will move back home. Maybe he will return to me, to the life we dreamed of. As we step off the boat he grabs my hand. "I have to piss so bad," he says. "That guy was so full of shit."

I got a teaching job in the fall of 2014. As part of earning my Master's degree in creative writing, I was able to teach an English composition class and reduce some of my tuition. I had never taught before, and with only a week of orientation and training, I felt extremely unprepared. I couldn't sleep the night before my first day of school, so I called my brother. We weren't speaking much at the time, even though I was back in Florida after a stint in Los Angeles, because I was afraid of getting close to him. When he answered the phone, he sounded so good.

We talked for hours about his experience as a teacher's assistant in grad school and he made me feel more comfortable about being in front of a room of "kids." I lay stretched out on my bed in my parents' apartment and listened to him tell stories and give advice. It was the closest I felt to him in years. I had been scared because I worried it wasn't possible to have a real relationship with him, like the one we had when we were little, the way things used to be, but could never return to because of everything that had happened. But it was nice, and it filled a void in my heart that I'd had for a long time. I had tried to replace him with the guys I dated, seeking a relationship like this, so close, so loving, but no one could replace him, no one was like him. It made me realize that our love was infinite, that I loved him like a kindergarten crush, intense and doting, thinking it would last forever.

On the last night we stumble upon a restaurant on the beach. We take off our shoes to enter and decide to sit at the bar because that is how you get drinks quickly. No one is taking our order though. There is a wedding out back of the restaurant and everyone is wearing white. We can't tell the servers from the partygoers. Everyone is drunk and dancing and we hear popular songs and joyous hollering. The bartender comes back and takes our orders and still forgets our drinks. I'm waiting on a tequila sunrise; he's waiting on something with whiskey in it, maybe even just whiskey on the rocks. Our food comes and the Mahi is the freshest I've ever had. The fries are curly and crispy and there's an aioli for dipping pleasure. He barely touches his hamburger because he wants his drink. Guests keep coming inside and asking for things; a straw, a cup of limes, a bottle of water, shots, more shots, napkins because they are sweating so much from dancing, and the bartender has orders to tend to the guests first. No one else is inside the place except for us. The food is delicious and I eat and watch the people dancing and singing. A wedding, a wonderful wedding for people who love each other and they invite their friends and families to watch and join and they all drive down across the rickety bridges and none of them throw apples into the Atlantic Ocean. A young couple comes inside drunk and sees our situation. Feeling badly they buy a round of shots that somehow gets made faster than our initial drinks and we take them. I feel good. I feel happiness here. People can be good. But his anger is growing. He wants his next glass. He wants more alcohol. I want him to think the wedding is beautiful, that the party is fun and everything is going to be okay. I want him to know that I love him but it's different now. I love him like a parent loves a child, sad and understanding, unconditional with the condition that he will never know what it's like to look at him here at this bar on this night, blue laser lights flashing, the dance floor, the nice couple, the fresh fish, the world spinning around and around all for us and knowing that it means nothing, that it is not good enough, that this is the last time I will ever see him because after this it truly is time to move on, to move forward, to keep my own world turning. His world is not meant to last forever.

When I was six I was given a fuzzy purple notebook. I wrote down everything that I saw and heard in that notebook. It became my best friend. I loved that it was purple, my favorite color, and fuzzy and had a latch to lock up all my secrets. I got it on the morning of a friend's birthday party. We were going to the city to see *The Nutcracker* and there was nothing Mom could do to stop me from bringing it. She told me to leave it in the car but I took it with me anyway. I was obsessed with jotting down my feelings, my fears, my everything.

I don't remember the play at all. I don't remember what color tutus the ballerinas wore. I don't remember the music. I don't remember the cake at the party, the ice cream, the goodie bags. I only remember opening and closing my book. I only remember writing down which girls I hated and how I felt so out of place at the party.

I started keeping a real diary when I was in high school. Our prep school required laptops, and I soon found myself jotting down daily notes of foods I had eaten, fights I was having with friends or family, emotions I didn't want to bottle up anymore, all in one document. Some of these entries became poems, some short stories, some deleted and forgotten. I was trying to pinpoint the moment I started to become depressed, the exact time in my life when I started overthinking everything and stopped feeling joy. From my research, it was somewhere between my first heartbreak and the time Skyler told me he wanted to die. The span of a decade. I was fourteen when a boy I met at my neighbor's house stopped returning my calls and I was twenty-four when Skyler committed to getting help for himself. Looking back, it seems like a flash, but like the lights we once shined into the sky, it will last forever. Those years were spent trying to save my brother, trying to replace him in relationships, trying to lose myself in others so I could find him. These essays, love letters to win him back. He is my perpetual motion machine. All he ever had to do to earn my love was to spin, spin.

The first time my ex came to my parents' apartment was a surprise. He had said he didn't want to be in a relationship, then a few days later called and said to go outside, to look at the moon. He was standing in the parking lot waving, holding flowers, asking if he could come up. On the way to the elevator Mom stopped me.

"That's euphoria," she said. "That's what you're feeling right now."

When we started dating my mom did not approve. She was certain that things would go wrong, as they did, but she had a motherly sense that I should move on. One day when he came over to go to the pool, she came downstairs and asked to speak with him, privately. I had been drinking and parked myself on a chair and drifted off to sleep. I could hear them talking at first, her asking him what his intentions were, him saying it's not so black and white, then just the ocean, the sound of sleep.

We ignore all advice and take a trip to Orlando only a few weeks after we'd met. It rains on the first day and we stay in bed and nap. In a month, he will move to Los Angeles and in a year I will follow. Many bad things will happen. We will fight in my apartment, in his apartment, in the street, in the car. We will see other people and not tell each other. He will lie and I will hold onto some of the lies, let others go. I will perpetually live in fear of the future, of my relationships dying, of my world coming to an end.

I brush his hair with my fingers and feel grateful to have a man in my life, someone who says he loves me. Everything is perfect, the way it should be, and I don't care what anybody else thinks. I know he will never hurt me. I am so sure of it.

Space Mountain

It is our favorite thing to do.

Once we hit Tomorrowland, we take off running. Our sneakers bounce off the Disney concrete. Past the mechanical chrome palm trees and the Mickey Pop ice cream stands, swerving at the Astro Orbiter. We keep sprinting, faster. I hurry my little legs to keep up with my brother. *One more boost,* I think. *We'll be there soon.*

We enter under the giant sign—*Space Mountain*—the queue swooping down toward the control board, mapping out our journey into space. The floor below it is covered with silver balls the size of Cabbage Patch Kids, and they lay out of our reach, leaving me to wonder what they're made of. Are they light like my Beanie Babies? Are they too heavy to carry like Skyler's Chrome Edition Buzz Lightyear?

From then on, it's a race. We zip past each other along the path. In the dark, we swing and climb the route, holding onto the metal bars lining the way, jumping up and down, power-ups. My shorts swish, my sneakers press. He always gets ahead, higher than me on the path, and I watch him ascend.

It is silent when we watch the eye of the hurricane pass. I am eight years old and my brother is thirteen. It is our first August in Florida and we are taking part in our very first hurricane. The power is out. The house is dark. Our parents light candles inside, but my brother takes a flashlight out to the driveway. He shines the light up into the sky.

"When you shine a light, it goes forever," he says.

"What do you mean?" I tug at my oversized sleep shirt, pulling it down to shield my knees from the wind.

"It bounces around in space for millions . . . billions . . . trillions of light years. Once you create the energy, it keeps going."

He quickly flashes the light on and off.

"That's too much! It's too much light going out there!"

"The galaxy can handle it."

I trust him, but I still wonder where the light went, when the storm will turn back.

I am too little to ride Space Mountain. My mom and I wait for my brother to return as we stand by the exit ramp. Beyond us, a space station themed gift shop where one can buy Disney pins and pens and autograph books and astronaut costumes and even freeze-dried ice cream. Over the years we've accumulated so much of these souvenirs, so much stuff to remind us of happiness that now sits in boxes in the closet.

Mom asks me what I want to do next, and I always point to the castle on the map, even though there is no ride or attraction there. I just want to go to the castle. To see it, be there, live there, stay a while.

She says, "Yes, we'll see the castle, and then we have to go visit Mickey!"

I continue studying the map, the colorful illustrations of the park. I find Tomorrowland, the big white tent.

"That's where we are! Skyler's in there now."

Then, always as if by magic, he appears. Up the escalator and down the hallway. He is always coming back to us.

He lights up outside the local theater. He has pre-packed weed into a cigarette. I keep looking over my shoulder, nervous. He doesn't seem to care.

"No one cares." he says. "I work here. Quit worrying."

"Okay."

"Last week I burned the popcorn, and there was a fire, and I'm still here."

He takes a few hits. He motions for me to come closer, hands me the weed cigarette. I'm afraid someone might see. I don't want to go to juvie as Mom always warns me, but I inhale and exhale with a laugh.

"I'm excited for the movie." I hand it back.

"Me too."

People walk by, but he just stares at them. They keep moving. He gets higher.

We are Disney people. The kind who go for any old reason: hurricane warnings, three-day weekends, holidays, "sick days" spent away from our prep school three hours south. The CD spins in the dark blue player on my lap. I only listen to *NSYNC or *The Marshall Mathers LP* in the backseat on the way up. My mom drives and talks to my brother about things I don't understand—Homecoming dance, applying for medical school internships, why dad is always gone. I lie down in the backseat and look out the window, a constant stream of telephone poles against a colorful sky. I try to name all the colors in my head—baby blue and robin's egg, lavender and violet, a slight string of light pink. My mother drives, my brother says something funny, and I fall asleep until we get there.

My brother walks around school with his sunglasses on, drinking a Coca-Cola. He only walks in straight, definitive lines. He's too smart and only has to take two classes a day. After that he can walk to his car and go home, or wherever he wants to go. Sometimes, like now, I see him walking across the Four Hundred building. I step out of my classroom to get a drink of water, or to just get out for a second because I hate school, I don't like what someone said to me that day, or I don't like feeling how I do, and I see him walking.

He's my hero, getting to leave school early, before it's over. He's even graduating a year early. He doesn't see me, but I watch him and wish I could walk next to him, be with him, leave with him.

The walls are lined with tubular windows that look out into space as I follow my brother up. Constellations on the ceiling twinkle and spin as rockets fly by. I always read the safety warnings. Even though none of them pertain to me, I think maybe someday they could—pregnancy, high blood pressure, other conditions that could be "aggravated" by this adventure. If something bad happened, which one would it be?

When I was too small to ride, my brother would stuff tissues into my Sketchers to make me taller.

"I need to get up there."

"You will, we can do it," he would always say.

I'm seventeen, and I take some friends to the movies. We smoke in the car on the way, and I put saline drops in my eyes to shrink the red when I park. My brother says he can get us in for free. We walk up to the window, and he's there in his suit jacket a few sizes too big. His hair is a little longer than usual. Jet black tufts fall in his eyes. He looks like he might be asleep. I knock on the window. He jolts. My friends laugh. I step closer. *Hey, it's me.* He's sweating. He wipes it off his forehead with the back of his sleeve. The sweat keeps pouring. His lips are cracked. He leans up on the microphone and struggles for a breath of air.

"Are you high?" he asks.

Once we get to the loading zone, my brother and I plan our seats. He says the back goes the fastest, insists we get rows five and six. I agree. I want to go as fast as possible, I tell him. In truth, I'd be happy riding the Tomorrowland Transit Authority PeopleMover all day. I'd be happy slowly inching my way through the park. I don't tell my brother that, though. I just stand on top of the number five and wait for the next car.

When it comes, we sit and the lap bar lowers down. The shuttles hold six people, single file. They are gray and white with dark blue cushioned seats. He sits behind me in the back and makes sure the flight attendants don't press his lap bar down too far. I always make sure mine clicks down to the maximum depth to hold my body in tight.

"Space shuttle, this is flight safety. Please keep your hands and arms inside the car, and remain seated while in motion. You are clear for launch."

I can't sleep. His room is across the hall from mine, and I can see a blue light glowing from the TV screen. His door is cracked open, and I go in. He's at his desk with a full bowl of plain Chex. His hand lingers over the bowl.

"What are you watching?" I ask from the doorway.

"*Neon Genesis Evangelion.*" He sits up, startled, then settles back. "Want to see something?"

He brings me over to his wall of Lego sets. There is a set staged with pirates fighting, and he picks up a small brown treasure chest from the scene. He pops it open. Inside are a few different colored pills: yellow, green, blue.

"What are those?"

"Oxys, the most amazing thing ever. Don't tell Mom and Dad."

"What is this show?"

"It's about the end of the world. It's a Mecha show. This boy was chosen by an organization named NERV to control a giant machine called an EVA to fight off the Angels. It takes place in an apocalyptic Tokyo."

He moves to his bed. I follow and sit on the edge.

"Look at the fucking moon, Britt."

A giant moon glows on the screen. A symphony plays and a boy inside a machine fights. I want to understand it but I don't. I want to trust that he knows what he's doing, like he always did, like he always does. He nods out. After a while, he falls asleep, and I shut off all the lights. I put the treasure chest back with the pirates. I leave the TV on. The blue light illuminates his room, the sound of symbols travels. I leave the door open.

We blast through a blue neon tunnel. A mirror at the end of the tunnel makes it appear infinite. We climb up at an angle, past the Mission Control Booth. Earth is a flat circle on the ceiling. Our shuttle shoots into the black: planets, stars, meteors, comets. We curve through twists and barrel down hills, we drop with speed into the silence.

Some friends are over on the weekend. We roll a joint in my room, and they ask if my brother will come outside with us. I knock on his door. He's there in his pajamas:

plaid pants and an oversized L.L.Bean t-shirt, torn-up and barely hanging onto his body. He throws on a sweatshirt and comes outside.

We smoke on the sidewalk and walk down to the cul-de-sac. The December air is cool, especially for Florida. I start to get dizzy. My friends leave, and I go back to my room. I sit on the edge of my bed and feel like I'm falling, dropping, dying. I can't breathe. I'm sinking into the room. My room is a box, and I'm shut inside. I can't tell anyone the secrets. I'm fixed in fixation. I'm the reason. I want to explode. I feel the space between my room and his. I feel the heaviness of my body drifting to the floor. There's no gravity in outer space. *It's just an illusion,* I think, *I'll be there soon.*

I float to his room, and the door appears locked. I start to cry in silence. My tears shatter the space. I slump down in the dark against the door. It opens.

He's at his desk, making lines of cocaine with credit cards. He looks at me like he knows something, like he wants to tell me something. I wait there for what feels like forever. His eyes are blank.

The ride finishes in a red swirling wormhole that turns black and globular. The shuttle slows down as we turn into the Space Port. I am breathless, ready to go again.

He tells me about the supermoon. He says to look outside tonight, another summer night at my part-time job over college break, and I'll catch it.

In between taking orders from a table and pretending to take a smoke break, I go outside. I search for the moon. I walk farther away from the restaurant and imagine my brother on his balcony in Aventura, standing there with a pack of Marlboro Reds, burning through each one as the blue sky fades to black.

My manager shouts at me from the back door. "Where are you going? What are you doing?"

I slip into the parking lot, beyond the rows of cars. My walk turns into a jog, then a run. I need to see it. I must find it. It is my mission, my debt to him, because I can't tell him what it means to be his sister, but here in the night sky I can be with him for as far as I can reach.

The moon rises above the trees. I see it glow. I watch it radiate.

The lap bar comes up. He jumps out first. I climb out after him, always trailing right behind.

I'm twenty-two. I take too many Oxycodone the first time I try them, a bottle left over from an eye surgery that I kept, just in case. It's my senior year, and my friends are out on the porch drinking. One of them gets an incoherent text, so she comes inside. I tell her to call my brother.

She calls him and puts me on the phone. He's not mad or scared. He understands. He says, "You'll be okay. Just try not to fall asleep. Eat something, anything, and get outside, get air."

I wish I could walk upstairs and go to his room and play *Mario Party* for a couple hours, like I did the first time I ever got high. He kept me company, nursed me back down. I feel far away from my body. I've lost my mind somewhere in this house. It doesn't seem right here: the brick staircase, the wet leaves on the ground, the smell of Svedka and Bud Light.

I think he says, "Get up," but it's, "Go outside." He says I can call back if I need to, but I don't. I sit outside on the porch for a long time. I stay there until it gets dark. I stare up into the black.

We step out of the shuttle. A moving platform takes us up, past a display from the Tomorrowland Express. The platform takes us back to Earth, where our mother is waiting. She's standing outside of the gift shop with our jackets hung over her arms. In a few years, the ride gets remodeled, shuts down for months, and Tomorrowland becomes a spot we will pass over. There even comes a time when we no longer go to the parks at all. But for now, we see our mom and run toward her, her bounce of blond hair, bright pink lips.

She smiles, asks us how it was. We always want to do it again.

Biographical Note

Brittany Ackerman is a writer from Riverdale, New York. She earned her BA in English from Indiana University and graduated from Florida Atlantic University's MFA program in Creative Writing. She is a Critical Studies instructor at AMDA College and Conservatory of the Performing Arts where she teaches Archetypal Psychology, Applied Logic and Critical Thinking, and Creative Writing. She was the 2017 Nonfiction Award Winner for Red Hen Press, as well as the AWP Intro Journals Project Award Nominee in 2015. She currently lives in Los Angeles, California.